Dec

Me   n

d hope neither you
nor your children
look like the characters
in this book – But
have as much fun
as they do!
  Lots of luck!
       x Caroline

More
Dad Stuff

A new shedload
of ideas for dads

by Steve Caplin and Simon Rose

SIMON &
SCHUSTER

London · New York · Sydney · Toronto

A CBS COMPANY

First published in Great Britain by Simon & Schuster UK Ltd, 2007
A CBS Company

Copyright © 2007 by Steve Caplin and Simon Rose
Illustrations © 2007 by Steve Caplin

The right of Steve Caplin and Simon Rose to be identified as authors of this
work has been asserted by them in accordance with sections 77 and 78 of the
Copyright, Designs and Patents Act, 1988.

1 3 5 7 9 10 8 6 4 2

Simon & Schuster UK Ltd
Africa House
64–78 Kingsway
London WC2B 6AH

www.simonsays.co.uk

Simon & Schuster Australia
Sydney

A CIP catalogue record for this book is available from the British Library

ISBN-10: 0-7432-9540-4
ISBN-13: 978-0-7432-9540-6

Typeset by Steve Caplin
Printed and bound in Great Britain by Mackays of Chatham Ltd

Contents

This book is dedicated to our children: Joseph, Izzy and Connie Rose, Freddy and Joe Caplin, who are all two years older and immeasurably wiser since *Dad Stuff* came out. And, of course, to their mothers, Jane and Carol, who have put up with all our experiments with unfailing good humour.

Thanks to all those who shared their knowledge, in particular:
Ian Carrick, Martin Ash aka Sam Spoons, Heather Ging, Pip McKerrow,
Mike McClean, Fiona Tracey and Charles Clarke
And those who sent suggestions through the Dad Stuff website:
Al Napp, Sam Roberts, Geoff, Rob Hallas, Chris Wiggins, Mark Y,
Dave Mackeral and Andy R

Need more? Meet the authors and other Dads to suggest techniques,
exchange tips or just chat about the whole Dad thing:

www.dadstuff.co.uk

Introduction

SHORTLY AFTER *Dad Stuff* was published, we received an email from a reader who pointed out that we'd made a mistake. In our handy guide showing the difference between a frog and a toad, a crocodile and an alligator, and African and Indian elephants, we'd mixed up bactrian camels and dromedaries.

Unfortunately, the book had already been printed. There was no way we could recall thousands of copies and paste erratum slips into the relevant pages, even using child labour (our kids). Somehow, we had to let the great British public know that a bactrian (Asian camel) has two humps, and a dromedary (African camel) has one.

There was nothing for it but to write another book containing this valuable information. We could have left it at that, of course, but our publishers thought sales might be higher if we put interesting stuff on the other two hundred odd pages as well.

So here it is: *More Dad Stuff*, which picks up where *Dad Stuff* left off. We've had countless new suggestions for tricks, tips and pastimes, both from friends and from visitors to our website: and, as our own children have got older in the intervening couple of years, we've become more skilled at answering those tricky questions that that are lobbed at Dads by their offspring.

This time, we've included a couple of slightly more serious chapters. One is *The behaviour thing*, which addresses the problem of managing children's behaviour. We've all read the behaviour chapters in those endless childcare books that grandparents lavish upon us the moment our children our born. The trouble is, most of these books assume that we have near-perfect children who are rational, obedient, and eager to please. This chapter is a behaviour guide for the real world.

We've also included a chapter called *Teach your children how to think*. It features a lot of the sort of puzzles that were so popular in *Dad Stuff*, but this time we outline the steps needed to help your kids arrive at the correct answers. Children's brains – unlike Dads' – are almost infinitely expandable: it only needs a nudge every now and again to set them in the right direction.

More Dad Stuff has been hugely enjoyable to write, both for us and for our children. We hope you'll get as much pleasure out of it as we did.

Steve Caplin and Simon Rose, London, 2007

Who's got the hump now?

Bactrian Camel (B has two humps)   Dromedary (D has one hump)

1 Rainy days and Sundays

SUNDAYS AREN'T WHAT they used to be. Time was, the day would stretch out endlessly before us, with nothing to do but hang about with our parents. Now, of course, Sundays are just like Saturdays, and are largely devoted to shopping.

But we can still find ourselves at a loose end at home on a Sunday – or on any day when it's too wet, cold and miserable to play outside. These are the times when a Dad's resources are most tested: sure, you can just plug the kids into the latest DVD rental, but there's a lot of fun to be had that doesn't involve TV screens.

You don't need much equipment to entertain bored children. We've assembled a range of games, activities and building projects that can be completed using everyday household items.

Of course, it helps to stock up on the essentials: a packet of balloons, a set of marbles, and the usual array of old cardboard boxes, sticky tape and glue. It doesn't take much organisation to provide an entertaining afternoon for your kids.

Camera games

Most of us have either a digital camera or a phone that's capable of taking pictures. There are many great games you can play with these: here are a few of our tried and tested favourites.

Spy camera

Our favourite games for a Sunday afternoon are those which involve the kids rushing around while Dad stays sitting in an armchair. This one requires only a small amount of initial Dad activity.

Take your mobile phone and half a dozen toy soldiers. Position the soldiers in various positions around the house, in plain view but tucked into unlikely places. They should be visible without opening drawers, but not so obvious they can be seen immediately.

Photograph each one in location with your phone, then show each of the photos in turn to your kids: their task is to locate each of the soldiers. If you prefer, just give them your phone and let them get on with it (but don't be surprised if they spend the whole time phoning their friends in Australia).

Taking extreme close-up views of their location makes the job much trickier, though occasionally it can be too difficult. We've found a good alternative is to photograph each soldier with a fair bit of background (enough to give the game away) on your digital camera. Then, when you show them back the images, begin with them zoomed all the way in. If they don't get the location straight away, you can zoom out step by step until they're able to tell where the soldiers are hidden.

Spot the body

Give each child your phone or camera in turn, and tell them to go off into another room and photograph part of their body. (You may need to censor the photos before general viewing takes place, just to make sure none of them have taken the kind of pictures that could wind you up in prison.)

When all the pictures have been taken, show them around: the task is to guess whose body each photo belongs to. It helps if you can rig your phone or camera up to a TV so they are large enough for everyone to see them.

Photo scavenger hunt

Kids seem to get their own mobile phones or digital cameras at a frighteningly early age these days. We tried pointing out to our kids that *we* didn't get our first mobile phones until we were in our thirties, but it didn't wash.

If you have a bunch of kids who all have their own phones, you can organise a scavenger hunt for them. Prepare a set of tasks to complete: they have to take a photo to prove they've done it. If not all the kids in your party have their own phones, organise them into teams with at least one phone or camera present on each team.

Depending on the age of the children, you can gauge whether to send them on tasks that involve leaving the house. Here are suggestions for some of the activities they could be asked to photograph:

- four of them on a zebra crossing, *Abbey Road* style

- as many kids as can fit in one bath/armchair/under a bed at one time

- standing on one leg, holding each others' free feet

- wearing hats, coats and sunglasses backwards

- pulling the silliest faces they can

- shaking hands with someone in uniform

- wrapped up in newspaper

- acting out a scene from a movie they all know

- scoring a goal with a balloon football

Climbing the wall

We all remember that old Batman series, where Batman and Robin would appear to be climbing a wall with a bat rope: in reality, the wall was built on the floor and the camera was tilted on its side.

It's a great time filler, and easy to do. Choose a clear piece of floor that could pass for a wall, and have your kids make as if they're having great difficulty climbing it – while you film them, with your camera held on its side. If you can make a fake window from pieces of wood or cardboard, it will greatly add to the effect. A perfect afternoon's entertainment with a video camera.

Being a pawn was bad enough – now I'm just cannon fodder

Chess combat

This is a game Steve invented when he was a student, and he's been playing it ever since. Take an old chess set that you don't mind getting a little battered, and arrange all the pieces clustered around the king, one colour at each end. Make sure all the pieces fit within an area four squares wide, so you have room on each side of them.

Stack books on end down each side of the board to catch stray pieces. If you can find some large sheets of cardboard, use these as walls at each end as well; hold them up when it's not your turn to fire, and take them down when it's your go.

It's now your task to knock over your opponent's king (and any other pieces in the way, of course) by flicking your pawns at it from behind the baseline. The trick to doing this is to press your index or middle finger against your thumb, *in contact* with a pawn: that way, when you release your thumb, it won't hurt your finger. If it isn't in contact with the pawn at the start, the act of hitting the pawn will hurt after a while. Take it in turns to fire pawns at each other's chess pieces. The board will quickly fill up with fired pawns and fallen pieces, but don't be tempted to take them off: the only 'rule' is that all casualties must remain on the battlefield. The added confusion caused by so much debris littering the board makes the game more fun as it progresses.

If you run out of pawns, you're allowed to stand up and fire any pawn on your side of the board – but you have to fire it from where it is lying. It's a raucous game, and marginally less mentally taxing than real chess.

There are two skills to this game. One is learning how to fire the pawns accurately, and the other lies in working out the best defensive placement of your pieces.

One word of recommendation: when a pawn flies off the table, as it surely will, stop the game and find it immediately. Otherwise you run the risk of losing a great many pawns very quickly indeed.

Tutty's Bulletin

A while back we heard of this great game, played in an office in Hull. It appears that there was a stationers, Tutty's, which produced a newsletter considered somewhat tedious by the employees of one office. So they formulated a game, the aim being to 'give' the newsletter to a colleague without them realising.

It might be secreted in their coat before they put it on, or in a file that they might then pick up. Cue giggles all round as the mark realised that they had unwittingly taken possession of Tutty's Bulletin. Apparently, so popular was the game that it has kept going for over twenty years, being passed from generation to generation of new office workers.

We think a family version would work wonderfully. You need to find something very distinctive and relatively easily concealed, such as an oddly coloured handkerchief or a peculiar toy or figurine. Somebody must be present when the object is discovered for a point to be scored.

If the mark discovers the object when they *aren't* observed, they can go on to hide it on or among the possessions of somebody else. We've both started the games in our households, though we don't honestly imagine that we'll be able to keep it going for anything like twenty years. But who knows? Maybe we will still be playing it with our grandchildren.

Peatime pickup

Although it sounds like a recipe for disaster, we're assured by very good friends of ours that a handful of annoyingly boisterous young children can be occupied for some time if you empty a big tub of dried peas, or something similar, onto the floor. Each child should be given an identical-sized container and a prize offered to the one who gathers up the most number of peas.

Retire to an armchair somewhere far away with the paper and a cup of tea as they compete to see who can get the most into their container. If it doesn't work, blame our chums, not us, and get out the Hoover.

This isn't doing our viewing figures any good

Don't watch that, watch me

We all know how compelling TV is for kids – but here's a way to make a game out of them *not* watching it, while teaching them just how compulsive the moving image really is.

Face your child, with the TV to the side of you. Look at each other's eyes. The game is to see who can hold out the longest without turning to look at the screen. It's much harder than it might seem, especially if the sound is left on: while it's just possible to ignore what's going on at any one time, as soon as the scene changes the need to see what's going on will quickly become unbearable. Give them a prize if they manage a minute!

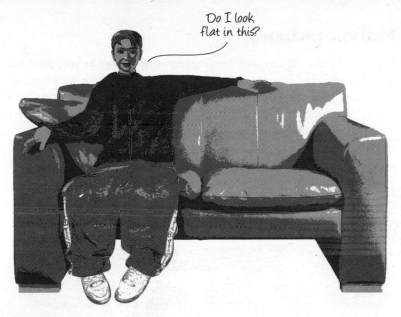

Flat people

If you want clothes that make you look thinner, this is the way to do it.

Get the kids to arrange an outfit of clothes – top, trousers and shoes, with gloves for the hands – on a sofa or chair so that when they go behind the furniture, it looks as though they're a two-dimensional person. It works particularly well when you view it later as a photograph. This is so quick and simple to do that it's now one of our firm favourites.

Spin things out by getting a group to compete to see who can come up with the worst or most outrageously dressed flattie they can.

Bicycle noises

Split a few drinking straws lengthways, then cut them into 2cm long pieces. Slot them around the spokes of a bicycle wheel, and they'll make a great rattling noise as they slide up and down while your kids ride along.

For even more noise, tape a piece of stiff card to the rear frame so that it scrapes on the spokes of the back wheel as they cycle. Sounds just like the motorbike they've always wanted – with the advantage that the card should wear out before the noise begins to drive you crazy.

Balloon games

Wonderful things, balloons. You can fart with them, make electricity with them, juggle with them and even skewer them without bursting them. As well as the ideas here, you'll find more balloon fun on pages 31, 42, 43 and 48.

Balloon whoopee

Farting always seems good for a laugh, not only with children, but most adult males too. Unless you're blessed with the melodic talents of France's one-time Moulin Rouge star, Le Pétomane (or 'The Fartiste'), you may need to improvise. While nothing can match the rich, deep rasping of manufactured whoopee cushions (except, of course, the real thing), you can still have a merry time with an ordinary balloon.

Simply snip off the ribbed end, keeping as much of the tube as you can. Blowing up the balloon is much harder without it but it can still be managed. Try, if it isn't too disgusting, to get plenty of moisture into the tube. Let the balloon go down, holding the tube between your thumb and index finger with varying pressure until you get a 'note' that you like. Once the tube gets really wet and adhesive, you may not even need to hold it at all.

Do bear in mind, though, that it will need much more well-developed lungs than usual to inflate the balloon, so this may one trick better left to Dads. 'But the kids told me to do it,' will no doubt be your perfectly reasonable excuse later on.

Balloon power

If you've got a spare fluorescent bulb (either the new energy saving bulbs or the old-style strip lights) try this experiment, which needs to be conducted in pretty dark conditions.

Charge up a balloon by rubbing it on a jumper, and bring it towards the bulb. As it gets close, you should see it light up. With energy saving bulbs, if you rapidly move the balloon towards and away from the bulb you can get them to stay alight, albeit very dimly.

A fluorescent tube is full of mercury vapour. When electrons are supplied to the bulb with electricity, they cause the mercury vapour to emit invisible ultraviolet light. The white coating on the inside of the tube is composed of phosphors, fluorescent chemicals, which turn the ultraviolet light into visible light. Rubbing a balloon charges it up with electrons and it is these that the mercury vapour in the fluorescent tube are reacting to.

Another neat thing you can do with statically charged balloons is to attract bubbles. Blow them in the normal way and bring the balloon close to one and the bubble will change direction towards the balloon. You have to be very nimble or it will simply crash into the balloon and burst.

Piercing balloons: the improved technique

In *Dad Stuff*, we explained how, by first putting some sticky tape on the outside of a balloon, you could pass a wooden barbecue skewer or knitting needle through it. And indeed you can, though not without the occasional explosive mishap.

Poke skewer through thick rubber at top...

...and out through the knot

However, one of our readers pointed out that there's a more sensible method. Don't inflate the balloon fully, but make sure there's still a dark area opposite the mouth of the balloon. The fabric of the balloon is thicker here, and under less pressure; it should be possible to get a skewer through if you proceed with caution. Poking it back out through the knot should cause no problem.

Balloon football

Watching football is endlessly tedious, as most Mums will tell you. The only good bits are the action replays in slow motion. So here's your chance to relive that winning goal: a balloon will naturally move in slow motion. If you and your kids do likewise, you can bring grandstand action into your living room.

Balloon juggling

It's easy to make your own juggling balls. Cut the top and neck off six balloons, and fill three of them with sand. Stretch the remaining three over these, so the holes end up opposite the holes in the originals. Bingo! Juggle away!

Marbles

Although you rarely see marbles played now, it isn't so long ago that these small glass globes containing coloured shapes could keep children occupied for hour upon happy hour. The Ancient Romans and Egyptians had them, made from stone or clay, and marbles feature in Shakespeare. Our language still recognises their influence, with phrases in common parlance like 'losing your marbles' and 'knuckling down to it'.

Indoors

There are an amazing variety of marble games. The one we used to play indoors was usually for two, though up to four could join in. With the furniture left in place as obstacles, each player starts from the same corner and has one roll. Unlike some marble games, the marble isn't flicked but rolled from your hand.

In turn, the players roll their marbles, releasing them at the spot where they ended up, the aim being to hit their opponents' marbles, either winning them or scoring points depending on mutually agreed rules. If you hit a marble, you get another roll but you must 'play away' and can't hit an opponent on that shot. Some winning strategies include trying to hide behind furniture legs to ambush others, and tempting others to play their marbles too close to a wall where they'll be easier for you to hit.

He'll never find us here, lads

Outdoors

Outside, the most popular variants usually involve a circle (a stick of chalk is handy) up to ten feet across, depending on the age and skill of the players.

In Ringo or Ring Taw, two players decide who begins by 'lagging' – throwing marbles from one tangent of the circle ('the lag line') to see who can land a marble nearest to the opposite tangent ('the pitch line').

At the centre of the circle, a number of smaller marbles (which are known as 'ducks', 'mibs' or 'migs') are placed in the shape of a cross. Players must 'knuckle down', keeping one knuckle in contact with the ground as, with their thumbs, they flick a larger marble, known as a 'tolley', 'shooter', 'masher' or 'taw', from any point on the circumference of the circle.

The aim is to knock another marble out of the ring while keeping their own tolley within it. If they succeed, they take that marble and continue where their shooter came to rest. If their tolley goes out of the ring, however, while they score any marbles that were knocked out, their turn is over.

Play also switches to the opponent if a tolley stays in the ring but no marbles are knocked out of it. For the initial go, from any point at the edge of the circle, the opponent can aim at the marbles in the cross, at the rival tolley or at any stray marbles.

If their tolley is already in the ring, they play from that spot. If anyone succeeds in knocking their opponent's tolley from the ring but stay in it themselves, their opponent is out of that game and must relinquish the marbles they've won.

It should be established at the outset whether playing for 'fair', in which case marbles are returned to their original owners, or 'keepsies', where winners keep the marbles they've gained.

Among the many marble buzzwords are 'fudging' or 'hunching' (using your shooting hand illegally), 'cabbaging' (shooting from the wrong place) and 'histing', (not having your knuckle in contact with the ground).

The British and World Championships take place each Good Friday at the Greyhound Pub in Tinsley Green in West Sussex, as they have done every year since 1932. There are two teams of six, each with 49 marbles placed in the elevated ring. The captains see who starts by 'tolleying off', dropping their marbles from their noses, trying to get closest to the edge of the ring. The first team to get 25 points wins.

Coin games

Remember how you could keep yourself amused for hours at school with a few coins from your pocket? Pass the tradition on, reminding your kids they don't have to spend their pocket money the minute they get it.

Pitch and toss

Known in some unimaginative corners as 'coinie', this once common playground game is for any number of players. Everyone stands in a line facing a wall, each armed with a coin of the same value. The object is to throw the coins so they land as close to the wall as possible. It should first be established if coins must hit the wall first and bounce off or not. Points are won either for being nearest or for the first three with descending scores. The first to a certain total is the winner.

A different game, confusingly also usually known as Pitch and Toss, involves throwing two coins in the air from upturned fingers of the same hand. If the result is two heads, the thrower wins. Two tails (sometimes known as 'two bikes') is a loss for the thrower. If it's one head and one tail then nobody wins.

This was once such a popular gambling game among adults, particularly miners, that it was made illegal and discovery was punishable with heavy fines. It's even mentioned in Rudyard Kipling's famous poem 'If'.

Penny rugby

The playing surface should be a bench or table with open opposite ends so that a coin can fall without hindrance. The two players sit opposite each other. The first starts with a coin half on and half off the playing surface. Their aim is to get the coin into a similar position on the opponent's side of the table, partly off the playing surface but without falling off. The player should initially hit the coin smartly with the side of their hand. They then have one more go flicking it with their finger to get it into position. If they succeed, they get 5 points.

If the coin falls off, the opponent wins a point. If the player fails to get it to the edge with their two goes, the opponent takes their two attempts from where the coin ended up. If a player is successful in getting the coin over the edge without falling, there's a two-stage conversion process. First, they must lean across the table and, with their middle finger, flip the coin into the air and catch it either with that hand or by clapping their hands together, depending on house rules.

If successful, the opponent must use their hands to form a goal, with their little fingers down, index fingers touching horizontally and thumbs vertically up. The goal attempt is made by putting the coin between the player's thumbs. With their forefingers on the table, they must flick the coin up and try to get it between the two uprights above the crossbar, for which 2 points are scored. Some rules have it that the player must first spin the coin on the table, catch it between their thumbs and instantly try to score as before.

If you want to make the game really complicated, use three coins originally set up in a triangle with a single coin towards the attacking player. They must flick this to part the other two and then make a 'run' up the table, always flicking the nearest coin through the other two in an attempt to get one coin hanging off the opposite edge. If at any stage a coin goes off or a player can't get the nearest coin through the other two, their turn ends and the coins are passed to the other player for his turn.

In the soccer variation, the goal is formed with touching index fingers forming a crossbar and thumbs the uprights (or vice versa for more skilled players). Local variants may allow another finger to act as a goalie, defending the goalmouth. The goal attempt is made by flicking the coin along the surface. Before an attempt at goal is allowed, the player must first succeed in the flipping up of the coin or catch the spinning coin between their thumbs or even both.

These games usually finish when the school bell goes.

Coin football

Everyone knows that the true purpose of school benches, tables and desks is for playing coin games on.

We wasted days of our lives playing coin football while waiting impatiently for the invention of computer games. The ball is a penny, while the two players are each represented by a two-pence piece. Starting in the centre, the first player strikes the ball with his player three times in an attempt to get it into the goal, usually represented by a pair of books of similar dimensions.

Players can't score straight from the centre spot and if they miss the ball at any point, play passes to the other player.

Card games

Everyone has a pack of cards somewhere about the house. Here are some entertaining and exhilarating games for children of all ages that should postpone their interest in online poker for a while.

Racing demons

This boisterous card game is like a competitive version of Patience. You need as many packs of cards as there are players (three to eight is best) and each pack must have a different design on the back. Bearing in mind how frantic the game gets, it's best to use scruffy cards rather than the pack you're keeping for your next bridge evening.

Unless you have a large table, it's best to play on the floor. Each player puts their hands flat on the floor either side of their pack of cards. At the word 'go', each player – as quickly as they can – counts out twelves cards face down, putting a thirteenth face up on top. They then deal four cards face up in a line to right.

Players then go through the rest of their cards, three at a time. If anybody has an ace in front of them or turns one over, it's placed in the central playing area. Anyone with the two of that suit can then put it down, using only the hand that isn't holding their cards. But everyone is in competition with each other, so it's the first to notice and slam their card down who gets it away. Anybody completing a run of one suit, from ace to king, grabs the whole pile.

The game continues until one player gets rid of their pile of thirteen cards, though they may still have cards in their hand or on the floor in front of them. They call 'stop' and scoring begins. For calling 'stop' you get 10 points. You get 5 points for each pile you have won but lose a point for each floor card you haven't played.

Each player must then gather in all the cards they haven't played and set them aside. Then all the cards that have been played are gathered up and sorted into the different packs, adding the number you played to your score.

Racing Demons is usually played over several rounds. If a stalemate is reached and nobody can play any cards at all, which sometimes happens, house rules usually allow everyone to put the top card in their hand to the bottom before recommencing counting in threes.

Demolition

This is another game where you want to use an old pack of cards. You need a demarcated playing area. An old-fashioned square card table is ideal. If playing on the floor, it needs to be somewhere where you can mark out a circle.

All the cards should be spread out face upwards in the playing area, with somebody who isn't playing to act as a caller. The players sit in a circle around the cards, either at chairs if at a table or cross-legged on the ground. The caller announces a card and the players must quickly locate it and drag it off the table or out of the circle, using only one of their middle fingers.

Unless somebody is very quick off the mark, the chances are that more than one player will compete for a card. The caller is allowed to call out the name of another card at any time, so players who are in mid-tussle may suddenly switch their interest to another card they think they can snaffle without competition.

The winner is the player to collect the most cards.

Pack of animals

Players must name an animal and demonstrate the noise that animal makes. Each player in turn takes a card, placing it face up in front of them. If anyone puts down a card that is the same rank as another exposed on the table, that player must say what animal he or she is, but then make the noise of the player of the *other* card.

If they make a mistake, they must take all the cards on the table. Get it right, though, and the cards go to the other player. Play continues with the person to the left of whoever picked up the cards. The object is to have as few cards left in your hand as possible.

Cheat

Divide the pack equally between all the players. The aim is to get rid of all your cards. The first player places as many cards as they like face down, saying what the cards are – for example, 'three queens'. The next player has to place cards either above or below that one in value: such as 'two jacks', or 'four kings'.

Of course, if you have a king and another player calls 'four kings', you know they're cheating, so you call out 'Cheat!' You all then examine the pack: if they were cheating, they take the whole pack of face-down cards; if not, you take the pack yourself. Try to keep track of who's placing which cards!

The magic touch

A good magician never reveals his tricks. We must be lousy magicians, then. Here's a selection of easy-to-do but impressive tricks to amaze your kids.

Now you see it...

Some children have an amazing ability to make loo paper vanish (leaving you to discover the fact only at the crucial moment). But here's a simple trick you can do virtually anywhere with a square of it, or a tissue or paper napkin.

Scrunch up the sheet of loo roll into a little ball, keeping it hidden in your hands. Tell the child you want them to make it disappear, using only the power of their mind. Get them to blow on your hands and then ask them to concentrate as, moving your hands as if still scrunching it, you shake them about, moving them above their head or to one of their ears and back again. Do it more than once if you like. Ask them to blow on your hands once more and then open them up to reveal that the loo roll has gone.

The secret, if you can give such a label to something so ludicrously easy, is to use the momentum of your hands moving out of their line of sight to drop the loo roll behind them. For that reason, the trick only really works on a one-to-one basis. Naturally, the paper needs to be silent, so old-fashioned Izal squares won't do (did they ever?) nor will bog standard (sorry!) writing paper.

The vanishing coin

Sit at a table, facing your kids, with a coin in each of your upturned palms. Flip both hands over so they're face down on the table, then slowly lift the right hand: there's nothing beneath it. Then, with perhaps the odd magic word, reveal that the coin has reappeared beneath your *left* hand.

It's an easy trick, that requires only a tiny amount of practice. As you flip your hands over, throw the coin from your right hand to be caught beneath your left. It's easier than it sounds, and we haven't met a kid yet who's able to spot it flying through the air: this is a case of the quickness of the hand, quite literally, deceiving the eye.

Starter for ten

Using whatever mumbo jumbo and razzmatazz you choose, tell a child you can tell what date is on a ten–pence coin they produce from their pocket. You don't need to see it, just for them to hold it in their hands.

All you need do for this trick is remember to specify a *ten*–pence piece (better hope you've given them one in their pocket money) and the date 1992. This is when the smaller ten–pence pieces were introduced and, as a result, about half of all ten–pence pieces currently in circulation still date from then: you've got an even change of getting it right first time. Of course, this isn't a trick that can bear much repetition.

You could, of course, cheat and memorise the dates of any other coins you give them. But we would never suggest doing that. Then it wouldn't be magic.

The flicking coin trick

This is a neat trick that, once practised, needs no preparation and very little equipment, just a playing card and a heavy coin. A one-pound coin is fine, but it's actually easier to perform the trick with a two-pound piece and, what's more, it looks more impressive.

Clench one hand into a fist but with your index finger pointing vertically upwards. On this you must balance the playing card with the coin in its centre, ensuring that it is exactly over your finger tip.

Now you must flick the playing card away, leaving the coin in place on your finger. Although it *should* be possible to flick the card away lengthways, we've never managed it. But to us it looks just as impressive flicking it sideways. You must be careful, though, not to follow through on the flick so far that you hit the coin. Not only does it spoil the trick but it hurts, too!

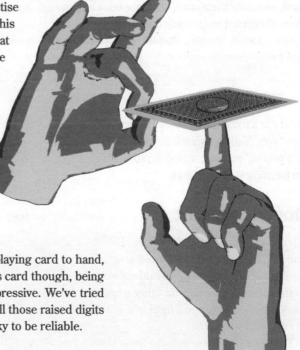

You'll need to practise a bit before you try this in public. Ensure that your flick is in line with the playing card and not pushing it up or down. The hardest part, to be honest, is not the flicking at all, but getting the two balanced properly on your finger.

If you don't have a playing card to hand, you can use a business card though, being smaller, it's not as impressive. We've tried with credit cards but all those raised digits make it a little too tricky to be reliable.

Pick a card...

Whether you shuffle the pack of cards in front of
your audience or not, before the magic commences
you must 'box' the pack by turning the bottom card the
other way up. Keeping that card in line with those above it,
fan out the rest of the cards with the faces downwards. Now you
get to say those truly magical words: 'Pick a card, any card.'

Let the child take the card and show it to anyone they like while you, as naturally
as you can, turn the pack the other way up in your hand. Thanks to the card you
turned over, it will look as though the pack is still facing down. Keeping the pack
together, ask your guinea pig to push the card back anywhere in the pack.

Get them to tap three times on the cards, muttering some hocus pocus if you
think it will help. Ask them to confirm their card with the others while you take the
chance to turn the pack over once more. Ask if they'd think it was magic if their
card, and only their card, was face up. Fan through the pack and, lo and behold,
there their card is, the only one facing upwards.

Don't forget, though, that the bottom card of the deck will also be face up, so
don't inadvertently show it.

...any card

Hold out a pack and tell them to pick a card, which they'll look at and keep hidden
from you. 'Tell me what it is,' you tell them. And they do.

'Correct,' you say, acting mystified that they aren't terribly impressed. There's
no pleasing some children.

Domino delight

Give your kids a set of dominoes. Tell them that you're going to leave the room,
and while you're out they must arrange all of them in a single line, so that the
number of spots on the right side of each domino matches the number on the left
of the following domino (in other words, as the game is played). Without coming
back into the room, you'll be able to tell them the number of spots on the dominoes
at each end of the line.

The trick: take one domino away before they begin. The spots will match the
domino you've taken. Sneaky, but very effective!

Greengrocer's grin

Sitting in a circle, everybody chooses a fruit or vegetable they'd like to be, the weirder and more exotic the better. A player must say the name they've picked twice, followed by that of another player's fruit or vegetable. That player must then say the name of their fruit or veg twice and then somebody else's once and so on and so on.

If any player shows their teeth, however, they are out of the game so – while keeping their own teeth hidden – players are also trying to make the other players laugh or otherwise lose their composure.

A variation of this is for the players, while avoiding showing their teeth, to name a vegetable that hasn't yet been mentioned, a progressively more difficult task.

Why is James wearing odd socks?

Give every player (there should be an odd number) a strip of paper and something to write with. Each person should write down a question beginning with 'Why?' about one of the other players. The questions are mixed up and handed out again, this time for everyone to write an answer to the question on the back.

A player should read out the question on their paper but the person to the left should read out the answer that's on the bit of paper they have. A little like consequences, the answers can be bizarre and occasionally surprisingly apt.

How did he die?

Players sit in a circle. The first person asks the second, 'Did you know Uncle Arthur died?' The second says, 'No. How did he die?' The first then chooses something about the death that the players can perform, such as, 'He died with one eye closed.' They must close one eye and keep it closed.

The second and third player now go through exactly the same exchange, ending with the second player closing their eye.

When it's the turn of the first player to speak again, they must add another trait, keeping the first one. Perhaps Uncle Arthur died, 'with one eye closed and screaming loudly' or with a stammer or shaking uncontrollably. Anybody getting it wrong as more and more of Uncle Arthur's unfortunately deadly afflictions are piled on, is out of the game. If course, if your kids *do* have an Uncle Arthur, you might like to change the name of this game to avoid complications.

2 Out to lunch: kids in the restaurant

ONE OF THE GREAT JOYS of seeing our kids grow up is that they can begin to participate in more adult activities with us. The day eventually comes when you can return to restaurants that serve real food, rather than burgers and chips hurriedly gulped between visits to the in-house ball pond.

Restaurants do have to be approached with care, of course. Even the most patient child will have trouble sitting still while waiting for their food to arrive. We favour beginning with restaurants that involve no waiting at all – such as those serving sushi on conveyor belts, or help-yourself buffets, or (our personal favourite) the kind of Chinese lunch venue where dim sum come round on trolleys.

There will come a time, though, when you've ordered your food, the drinks are with you, and you need to pass the time until your meals arrive. This is where Dad can shine: keeping kids amused and entertained in public is the sign of greatness. We've got a range of solutions to help you on your way, along with a more radical suggestion for when service is sluggish and you need to attract the waiter's attention by any means possible.

Games and puzzles

Nothing keeps a child's mind occupied as well as a puzzle. Here's a selection of diversions that are particularly good for playing in restaurants, as they need only the items to hand and cause the minimum amount of disruption.

The coin puzzle

An easy trick to reveal, but one which is hard to puzzle out. Take two pound coins, and place them about eight centimetres apart on the table (it *has* to be a table with a tablecloth for this trick to work). Place a thinner coin – 2p, 1p or 5p – between the two wine glasses. Now turn a glass upside down, and place it so it's resting on the two pound coins, with the other coin unreachable beneath the glass.

The challenge is to get the small coin out from under the glass without touching the glass or either of the pound coins. And that includes not touching them with cutlery, so if they try to slide a knife blade beneath the glass they'll lose when it tips the glass over.

The solution is utterly straightforward: simply scratch the tablecloth with a fingernail, directly in front of the glass. Each time you scratch the coin will creep towards your finger, until it eventually comes right out from under the glass.

Menu games

Kids choose quickly in restaurants: adults can take longer to compare the merits of each dish on offer. To keep them occupied while you make up your minds, have them search the menu for a particular word, or look for the most expensive item (but don't necessarily encourage them to order it). If you're in a posh restaurant, get them to find the most expensive bottle of wine – they'll be amazed.

There are endless variations on menu searches. You could assign them each a colour – red, brown, white and green are good – and have them search the menu to find as many items as they can that match their chosen colour. You may not ever get your children to *eat* their greens, but at least this way they'll get an idea of what they are.

A good menu game to play while you're waiting to be served is the Missing Words game: you read out a menu description, and they have to guess the one word you've missed out. It's going to be tricky if the missing word is 'coulis', or 'ganache', or 'fricassee', or any one of the dozens of fancy expressions restaurateurs use to justify their inflated prices; but it can be funny if, for instance, you're going through the children's menu item by item, and the one word you keep missing out is 'chips'. Remember, this is a game designed to amuse, not a challenge to test their culinary knowledge.

Fork balancing

Give your kids two forks and a toothpick. The challenge is to balance them all on the neck of an open bottle so that only the toothpick is touching the bottle.

You may want to clear a little space around the base of the bottle before starting this one, as in the first few attempts the forks are bound to fall. It's best if there's a tablecloth to muffle the sound of crashing cutlery!

The solution: first, knit the forks together so that their tines interlock. Press them together to make a firm joint. Then wedge the toothpick into the fork assembly so it holds hard. All you have to do now is to rest the toothpick on the edge of a bottle or a glass, and the cantilever action will make the forks stay in place, perfectly balanced.

If you're feeling really ambitious, try resting the forks on *two* toothpicks. Build the assembly with one pick, as described above; then place the second so it rests just inside the neck of a bottle, and balance the other toothpick (and the forks) on the other end. Amazing when it works!

What can we make at this restaurant?

A good waiting game is to see how many words you can make from the letters that make up the name of the restaurant you're in. It's an anagram game, but with a twist: your kids score extra points if they can make up items of food from the letters in the restaurant's name. Just in case you happen to be playing there, McDonald's contains all the letters needed to spell Almonds, Salmon, Damson, Clams, Soda and Cod.

An easy one if you happen to be in somewhere like The Hungry Hippo All You Can Eat Burger and Pizza Emporium, but a little tricky if you've ended up in a branch of Wimpy (and you should think yourself lucky that the only branches of Pizza Pizza are in Canada).

Some sort of prize should be given if a child manages to think up an anagram that uses all the letters in the name: McDonald's is an anagram of Damn Clods, for instance, and Hard Rock Cafe makes Fake Car Chord. (It also makes For Crack Head, but you might want to keep this to yourself.)

Lean on me

You'd never want to do this in a stuffy restaurant, but it can be great fun if your waiter has already established a bantering rapport with the children. You might also consider it if you've complained about the table being wobbly and feel that too little has been done to rectify the problem.

When the waiter is out of sight, use salt to raise one side of various objects such as place mats or the salt and pepper shakers, if they're of suitable design. The aim is to get several things on the table tilted at about the same angle. When the waiter returns, the entire family should be leaning in line, the aim being for everybody to behave completely normally – or at least what passes for 'normal' in your household.

In fact, the real struggle is not to burst out laughing almost instantly. Try going through the whole ordering process with the children and somebody – possibly you – is bound to giggle before it's done.

This Leaning Tower of People also works well when dining with your relatives, providing they have a good sense of humour. It could be ages before granny realises just what's odd about the scene around the dinner table.

Hot air wrappers

If you are ever *en famille* in an Italian restaurant that serves those lovely almond-flavoured amaretti biscuits, make sure you hang on to the thin paper they usually come wrapped in (though not the thick, waxy wrappers you occasionally get).

Shape the wrapper into a cylinder along its longer side and place it on a plate or saucer. Light the top of the paper. The flames will steadily burn downwards. Just before they reach the bottom of the cylinder, the lift from the hot air will be sufficient to float the delicate paper, still burning, several feet up in the air. Use the plate or saucer to catch the ash as it floats back down.

There can't be an Italian waiter anywhere who hasn't seen this trick and, having heard tell of smoke detectors being set off, perhaps it's best either to check first that the staff don't mind or else take the wrappers home and try it there.

If you never encounter amaretti biscuits, you can also use those teabags that come with a string attached. Remove the string and the staple that attaches it to the bag. Pour out the tea into the pot, after warming it of course, so you can have a nice cuppa.

Unfold the teabag and you will see that it's really a long cylinder. Keeping it as cylindrical as possible, place it on a plate or similar and light the top. It works almost as well, though you don't get to enjoy the lovely biscuits or the green or blue-tinged flames that come off the amaretti paper.

Pizza toppings

Each child has to make up a pizza, each ingredient beginning with successive letters in their name. Easy if their name happens to be Tom (tomatoes, olives, mozzarella); less palatable, but still edible, for a Martha (mushrooms, anchovies, radish, tea leaves, ham and apples).

Spare a thought for all the kids out there named Max and Zoe, though, as they'll end up gnawing their way through xylophones and zebras.

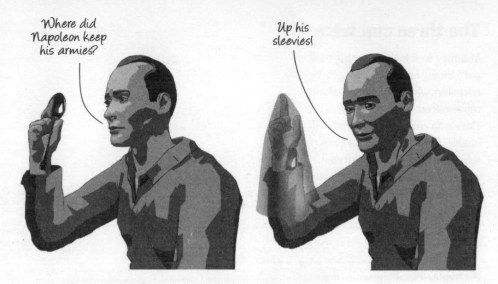

Where did Napoleon keep his armies?

Up his sleevies!

The amazing vanishing teaspoon

Table top magic is always appreciated, even when it's fairly obvious how the trick is done. Of course, the more bravado and stagecraft you can bring to this, the better it will go down. Check you aren't wearing a T-shirt *before* starting this trick.

Hold a teaspoon in your hand as shown, and cover your hand with a napkin (a cloth one will work best, if you're in a posh enough restaurant). As you put the napkin in place, let the teaspoon drop down into your sleeve; raise your forefinger to take its place, and it will look as if the spoon is still there.

Whip the napkin away with a flourish, folding your finger down as you do so – and ta-ra! The spoon has magically vanished!

Of course, you're now left with a spoon up your sleeve. Stand up, and pick up an empty glass from the table, using the hand that has the concealed spoon. Cover the glass (and your hand) with the same napkin, say a magic word, and allow the spoon to slip out into the glass with a magical chinking noise. Take the napkin away, and the trick is complete.

The three cup trick

You may well have seen this trick performed on street corners by tricksters who are expert in taking money from gullible passers-by. Here's an easy version which will enable Dads to win back pocket money from gullible children.

You need three clean cups and a pound coin. Don't be tempted to use cups that have had coffee in them, or you'll leave nasty stains on the tablecloth.

Turn the cups upside down on the table. Place the coin under one of the cups, and ask your kids to watch carefully so they can tell you where the coin is.

Shuffle the cups around at random, using both hands. Then, as you move the cup containing the coin forwards, tilt it away from you slightly so the coin slips out from behind it.

Keep on moving your hand and the cup forwards, and trap the coin beneath your palm. It should stay in place as you move your hand around the table top, as long as you don't move it too far. This is the most difficult part of the trick: make sure you do something flashy with the other hand at this moment, to distract attention from what you're really up to: perhaps waggle your fingers, or rattle the cup you're holding in it.

Then, while you switch to grasp a different cup, release the coin that's trapped under your palm. All you have to do now is to tip *that* cup forward as you pull it back, to allow the coin to slip underneath it.

Like all magic tricks, this one does benefit from some practice before you attempt it in public. It works best on a table with a tablecloth, which will muffle the tell-tale sound of pound coins scraping on wood.

Tippit

Apparently a Welsh game also played in parts of Europe, Tippit needs two teams of three, a table and a small coin. It's a good one for pubs and restaurants if there are enough of you, though we've also heard of it being played at parties and using marbles or nuts instead of a coin.

The coin is tossed to see who goes first. That team hide their hands under the table, passing the coin between them until, when they are ready, the middle player knocks on the table three times.

The players put their six closed fists – one of which contains the coin – on the table. The other side can confer amongst themselves as they try to work out which fist contains the coin. The middle one must name a player and say one of two things. They may order them to 'Take your right/left hand away' and the designated player must open that fist and, assuming there's no coin there, remove it from the table. If the coin *is* there, the team hiding the Tippit have won that round. They score a point and hide it again.

Alternatively the leader of the seeking team may point at a player and say, 'Tippit in your right/left.' That person must open their hand to show if the Tippit is there. If it isn't, the hiding team have won their point and have another go.

If, however, the Tippit is in the chosen fist, the seekers score a point and the coin passes to them, who now have to hide it. Tippit is generally played until one team has eleven points.

Tippit makes for a fun family game as players have to do their utmost to convince the seekers to pick the wrong hand, while those looking for the coin may indulge in staring contests in an attempt to make the hider of the Tippet crack under the psychological strain! Children not yet certain of the difference between their left and right will find they quickly learn. As with so many pastimes, it's easily adaptable into a drinking game when the kids have gone to sleep.

The barfing tomato

Get hold of a cherry tomato (one of those really small ones), and cut a horizontal slot in it. When you hold it in your hand, you can make it 'talk' by squeezing your fingers together.

Doing your best ventriloquist voice, make it say something like: 'I don't feel too good… must have been something I ate… oh, I think I'm going to throw up… here it comes… eeurgh!'

On the final 'eeurgh!', squeeze your fingers and thumb together and the tomato will barf its contents out of its mouth. Sounds disgusting, and it is. Which is why kids love it, of course.

This is so embarrassing

Peppercadabra

You'd think that if you mixed salt and pepper together, you wouldn't be able to separate them again without tweezers and a good deal of patience. So challenging your children to do just that should keep them occupied for a while.

Pour some salt onto a plate and then add a little pepper on top. The fine stuff that comes in packets is best but ground pepper will work too, just so long as the pieces aren't too big.

Naturally, separating them again is a trick. If you have a plastic comb, smarten yourself up by combing whatever's left of your hair a few times. It will cause static electricity to build up on the comb. Hold it over the salt and pepper and the static on the comb will pick up the grains of pepper, which are lighter than the salt grains. If you haven't a comb, anything else that will take a charge will do, such as a balloon rubbed on a jumper. Easy when you know how.

Food facts

A great Dad is recognised by his ability to pluck fascinating facts out of the air to suit any occasion. And few occasions are as good as being in a restaurant, when you have a captive audience eager for food-related trivia.

Pizza

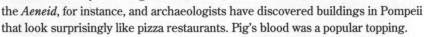

People have been putting food on discs of bread for thousands of years. Virgil mentions them in the *Aeneid*, for instance, and archaeologists have discovered buildings in Pompeii that look surprisingly like pizza restaurants. Pig's blood was a popular topping.

The version we have today, with a cheese and tomato base, was invented by Raffaele Esposito in Naples, in around 1830. His restaurant, Antica Pizzeria Port' Alba, is still serving pizza today.

In 1889 Esposito was commissioned to bake a special pizza for the visit of King Umberto and Queen Margherita of Savoy. He made it in the colours of the Italian flag – green, white and red – using basil leaves, mozzarella and tomatoes. You can still buy this concoction in any pizza outlet, and it's called a Margherita.

Hamburgers

Street stalls in ancient Rome sold cooked meat in ciabatta. In the 12th century the Mongol horsemen of Genghis Khan needed food that was easily portable, and which could be eaten with one hand while holding the reins with the other; they used to place ground-beef patties between the horses and the saddles, where they would be tenderised as they rode along. When Genghis' son, Kubla, invaded Moscow in 1238, the Russians were so impressed by their raw ground meat that they called it *Steak Tartare* (Tartar was the Russian name for a Mongol).

German ships visiting the Baltics brought the idea home with them, most notably to the port of Hamburg – hence the name, just as other German cities have given us Frankfurters and Vienna sausages. Hamburgers were never made of ham.

An early recipe for 'Hamburgh Sausages' was published in England in 1758 in *The Art of Cookery Made Plain and Easy*. Hamburgers were served between two pieces of bread, until Walter Anderson invented the burger bun in 1916.

Hot dogs

Sausages are one of the oldest forms of processed meat: Homer mentions them in the *Odyssey*. The hot dog as we know it was apparently invented in Frankfurt, Germany in 1487; the city celebrated the 500th anniversary of the frankfurter in 1987. The American National Hot Dog and Sausage Council (yes, there really is such a thing) asserts that the hot dog was invented by Johann Georghehner in the 17th century.

In the 1830s a rumour spread that stray dogs were rounded up and made into sausages, and frankfurters came to be called Dog Sandwiches. The 1860s song *Where oh where has my little dog gone* contained the following verse:

Und sausage is goot: Baloney, of course,
Oh where, oh where can he be?
Dey makes 'em mit dog, und dey makes 'em mit horse:
I guess dey makes 'em mit he.

In 1870 a joke appeared in American newspapers: 'What's the difference between a chilly man and a hot dog? One wears a great coat, and the other pants.' This is the first known printed reference to hot dogs.

Sandwiches

The first recorded sandwich was made by the rabbi Hillel the Elder in the first century BC, who started the Passover tradition of placing chopped nuts, apples and spices between two pieces of matzo.

Flat blocks of stale bread, known as trenchers, were used instead of plates during the Middle Ages. The bread absorbed the juices from the meat, and was then either eaten or, if you were feeling generous, tossed to a waiting peasant. Plates weren't invented until the 15th century.

So in 1762 when John Montague, fourth Earl of Sandwich, asked for his steak served between two slices of bread so he wouldn't have to leave the gambling table, he wasn't really inventing anything that new. But other members of his club began asking for their steaks 'the same as Sandwich', and the name stuck.

The Earl of Sandwich, incidentally, was a patron of Captain James Cook, who named the Sandwich Islands after him. They're now known as Hawaii. Cheese and pickle hawaii, anyone?

Drink facts

All kids love soft drinks – even if there are those of us who believe that the only appropriate drink in restaurants is tap water. Here are some facts that should help to pass the time before your food arrives.

Coca-Cola

In 1863, a Corsican named Angelo Mariani invented 'cocawine' – a mixture of wine and cocaine. It was copied by Dr John Pemberton in Atlanta, Georgia, who called

it Pemberton's French Wine Coca, using coca leaves as the stimulant. But when Georgia brought in Prohibition (the banning of alcohol) in 1886, Pemberton replaced the wine with a caffeine-based beverage made from cola nuts, and changed the name to Coca-Cola.

In 1903 the company started using 'spent' coca leaves (after the cocaine had been removed). They still use this formula today, and legend has it that only two top executives know the precise details – they're said to have half the formula each.

During the Second World War, the Coca-Cola company guaranteed to make its drink available to US servicemen anywhere they happened to be fighting. Of course, this meant building bottling plants all over the world – with US Army backing. When the war ended, the Coca-Cola company was poised for world domination.

The highest consumption of Coke per person in the world is in Mexico and, er, Iceland.

Pepsi

Invented by a chemist called Caleb Bradham in the 1890s, Pepsi was originally called Brad's Drink. He sold it as a cure for stomach pains, or 'dyspepsia' – which could explain the change of name. Bradham initially sold Pepsi as a syrup, which customers would dilute themselves.

Pepsico went bankrupt due to high sugar prices in 1923, and again in 1931. They introduced a 12-ounce bottle in 1934, double the size of the Coca-Cola bottle, under the slogan 'twice as much for a nickel'. Their company slogans have included 'more bounce to the ounce', 'be sociable, have a Pepsi' and 'now it's Pepsi for those who think young'. You can see why Coca-Cola have stuck with 'the real thing'.

Other soft drinks

Lemonade was first brewed in Egypt, over 1500 years ago, and was made with lemons and honey. The *Compagnie de Limonadiers* was formed in Paris in 1676, and had exclusive rights to sell lemonade from street vendors. In 1788, the newly invented 'Geneva Apparatus' allowed artificial mineral water to be created, which meant lemonade could be given its fizz.

7 Up is a lemon and lime flavoured fizzy drink first created by Charles Grigg in 1920. No one knows exactly where the name came from; some believe it to refer to the fact that the company had gone bust six times before the drink was invented. Whatever the origin, it's better than Grigg's original name for the drink – 'Bib-Label Lithiated Lemon-Lime Soda'. Catchy, we're sure you agree.

Ginger beer first appeared in England in the 1700s, and was made from ginger, sugar, water and 'ginger beer plant' – a slushy, thick white goo containing yeast and a special bacteria, which together cause the fermentation.

Tomato juice is made simply from squeezed tomatoes, and is the official state drink of the state of Ohio. It's mixed with beer in Canada and Mexico, where it's known as a Calgary Red-Eye or Cerveza Preparade; and with vodka, when it's called a Bloody Mary. Tomato juice is popularly believed to be useful in removing the odour left by skunks.

Perrier is the best known of the mineral waters. It comes from a spring in France called Les Bouillens, and was formerly owned by one Louis Perrier. He sold it to the English aristocrat Sir St John Harmsworth, who marketed it in green bottles shaped like Indian clubs. Perrier does come out of the ground fizzy, but not *that* fizzy: carbon dioxide (from the spring) is added later.

Dandelion & Burdock has made a recent revival since being sold in cans. But only in bottles can you see the rich dark colour that made it look like cough medicine but tasting so much better. Traditionally, this supposedly detoxifying drink was made from fermenting the roots of burdock plants and dandelions, but it's unlikely these days to contain any element of either. Americans tasting it would think it very similar to their sarsaparilla.

Disgusting food around the world

If your children insist that food set before them is gross or are fractious in a restaurant, it can be handy to remind them of some of the more unusual gastronomic treats savoured in other countries. If you're worried you haven't come out with enough money, it might even suppress their appetites, making it less likely that you'll end up in the kitchen washing dishes. If they're made of tough stuff and claim they'd love giant toasted ants or whatever, call their bluff – a surprising number of these delicacies are now available to buy online.

Japan: Ice cream flavours include squid, octopus, ox tongue, crab, shrimp, eel, raw horseflesh, goat, whale, cactus, shark fin noodle, chicken, seaweed, spinach, garlic, tulip, lettuce and potato and even silk.

Gold is a permitted food additive (E175). In Japan they add gold leaf to tea, and use it as a garnish on other dishes.

A poisonous puffer fish, a delicacy known as fugu (right), is 25 times more dangerous than cyanide. The poison is removed before serving; many deaths occur each year through inept preparation.

Watch it, mate – I'm a kung fu-gu

Indonesia: Deep-fried monkey toes are eaten off the bone. Smoked bats are a delicacy.

Thailand: Giant Bug chilli paste is a hot sauce made from water scorpions. Thais also eat rat, which apparently tastes a little like rabbit.

Among a selection of Thai delicacies for purchase on the web are edible roasted giant water bugs (left), bags of roasted scorpions, roasted giant crickets, roasted pregnant crickets, roasted meal worms and a can of smoky barbecue flavour canned scorpions.

South East Asia: Cats, dogs and monkey brains are part of a well-balanced diet.

China: Duck or pig blood is eaten in the form of a jelly. There's also a restaurant in Hunan province that uses fresh human breast milk in their recipes.

Scorpion toffee (right) is a big lump of amber-coloured toffee with a crunchy scorpion trapped inside. Specially bred to be eaten, they aren't poisonous. Or so the makers would have us believe.

Vietnam: Rats. Often the star ingredient in rat stew.

USA: In the south, cooked squirrel brains are eaten out of the skull. Apparently it's possible to catch mad squirrel disease from this! Several people have died.

Hungary: Freshly killed pig's blood fried up with scrambled eggs.

Ukraine: Pig fat eaten cooked or raw. Now available covered in chocolate.

Sweden: Blood dumplings. Made of flour, reindeer blood and salt, they're served with bacon, butter and jam.

France: Frogs legs, snails and horse meat.

Europe: Black pudding (left), also known as blood sausage, boudin, morcilla de burgos and blutwurst. Whatever the name, it's made from congealed blood, fat and offal.

Spain: Criadillas, or bull's testicles (also known as Prairie Oysters in Canada).

Mexico: Chahuis (right) are the worm-like insects that feed on the mesquite tree, and they're commonly found in bottles of tequila. You can also buy them, roasted, to eat as a tasty snack.

Great Britain: Barbecue flavour crispy worms. Also crocodile curry, ant lollies, chocolate covered scorpions, giant toasted ants and our favourite – coffee that's been eaten and regurgitated by weasels. Well, OK, these may not be native foods to this country, but you can buy them all here through www.lazyboneuk.com. Well worth a visit!

More unusual food facts

Here are some more unusual facts about food that might help pass the time while you're waiting for your waiter to nip get back from Italy (which is clearly where he's gone to get the pizzas you ordered).

While an apple a day is said to keep the doctor away, apple pips actually contain cyanide, the stuff murderers seem to have elected as the poison of choice, if Agatha Christie is to be believed. Some people seem terrified of apple pips as a result but in fact your digestive system could quite happily cope with the absolutely tiny amount of poison each pip contains. Even a lot wouldn't harm you, particularly as your stomach's acids would have trouble eating through the protective coating. If apple seeds weren't so hardy and were digested in animals' stomachs, there wouldn't be nearly as many apple trees.

Incidentally, peach and cherry stones contain cyanide too, so don't go eating too many of those either. And while we're on dangerous foods, cassava – the root tapioca comes from – is chock-full of the stuff, but it's rendered harmless in the preparation.

Although avocado's a pretty popular fruit these days, don't give any to your pets. All the bits of the avocado, including the flesh we eat, contains persin which, while causing no problems to people, is poisonous to a wide variety of animals, including birds, dogs, fish and rabbits. So no dropping guacamole into the dog's bowl to get out of eating it.

Tarantula spiders are found periodically in boxes of bananas in supermarkets. These so-called banana spiders get transported here despite the bananas being washed, sprayed with fungicide and inspected as they're packed. Creepy crawlies

Makes a change from water spouts

they may be, but they're usually harmless to humans. Very occasionally poisonous black widow or other spiders turn up alive in the veg section of supermarkets, though they're usually killed off by the refrigeration used to keep the fruit and veg from going off.

Contrary to the urban myth, the black bits in bananas are not tarantula eggs. They're the remnants of banana seeds, which have been bred out of the fruit to make them more palatable.

3 Sleepover and party games

IF ANYBODY INVENTED the sleepover, they're not owning up to it – probably because they're petrified that countless sleep-deprived parents would want to have a quiet word with them.

Loathe them or hate them, though, sleepovers are now common, particularly among girls. Depending on their age, supplying them with tried and tested games to play can be a good way of keeping down the level and longevity of the inevitable mayhem.

All kids love parties, especially if it's their birthday. But running a successful party involves more than just making sure you've remembered to get the right number of candles for the cake: you need to plan exactly what the little darlings are going to be doing if you want to avoid them rampaging through the house and destroying your prized ornaments.

We've put together a fantastic selection of activities and games that should keep them happy and busy – some involving rushing around expending energy, some more sedentary.

Oh! Where's everybody gone?

The Funky Chicken

This group activity, which works best with large numbers, needs to be initiated by an outgoing child or a Dad utterly lacking in the embarrassment gene. Whoever leads it off starts by shouting out 'Chicken' loudly. Then, imitating panto chickens, they continue by chanting in a sing-song manner:

Chicken with a wing	(flapping their elbow like a wing)
Chicken with two wings	(flapping both elbows)
Chicken with a leg	(lifting and shaking a leg)
Chicken with two legs	(doing the same with both legs in quick succession)
Chicken with a head	(imitating a chicken's pecking action)
Chicken with a tail	(turn and shake your bum)

Chicken chooses YOU.

At that point, they should select somebody else who should come and join in as the chant is repeated, at the end of which the new person picks the next until, before long, you have a massive group imitating chickens. The moment for playing The Funky Chicken needs to be chosen carefully. It can be a little unnerving if the first person goes through all that only to find that nobody else will join in.

Simon's daughter Izzy says she once did The Funky Chicken with a group of bored Girl Guides in Trafalgar Square, dragging hapless tourists into the action. Proof, if any were needed, that it isn't only Dads that embarrass their children, but that it works the other way round too.

Little Miss Noisy

The players group themselves in a circle around the person chosen as 'It'. 'It' is blindfolded and counts to ten slowly, allowing the other players to swap positions. 'It' should then point and the player indicated should make noises of any sort but without speaking, trying to keep their identity secret. If 'It' guesses who it is, that person then becomes 'It'. If not, the game continues.

Instead of the blindfold, of course, the game can be played at night with the lights out. What's most important, of course, is that this is played in a group where all the players know each other pretty well. If they haven't even been introduced, the game could go on for an awfully long time.

Hide and seek

Children hardly need any instruction on how to play hide and seek. It remains a favourite and, in these days of declining educational standards, parents may even take pride in their child's ability to count up to a hundred. But there's a super variant that works well at sleepovers for younger children as it's confined to just one room, a bedroom being ideal.

Making sure that anything sharp or fragile is safely out of the way, one of the players is blindfolded and then has to tag others in the room. Instead of hiding in the traditional sense, players try to keep out of 'It's way while at the same time teasing them by making noises and tapping their shoulder from behind and so on. If anyone is touched by 'It' they are out and must gather in one place, such as on a bed.

It sounds simple, and it is, but it's also amazingly good fun and can lead to delighted hysterics. On second thoughts, maybe it *isn't* the best game for a sleepover.

Balloon forfeits

Into balloons should be pushed rolled-up slips of paper on which are written assorted forfeits. For younger children, parents might want to make suggestions such as making noises or behaving like particular animals, singing songs, acting out adverts and the like. Older children may prefer to come up with their own devilish ideas.

The balloons should be blown up and then handed out randomly. Players take it in turns to sit on the balloons until they burst and must then carry out the forfeit. An added twist, rather than read out what's on the paper, is to ask the other players to guess what the forfeit says from what is happening.

Sleepover souvenir

The problem with sleepovers is that they're over all too soon – unless you're the sleep-deprived parents of course. It's very easy to conjure a long-lasting memory of the night, though, by getting everyone to sign a message on a light coloured pillowcase. If you're really organised you can tie-dye it first, otherwise simply hand over an indelible marker or two. You can use dedicated laundry markers if you like, but it doesn't really seem to make much difference.

The inscriptions really do last. We've got one or two dating back several years that don't seem to have faded at all and are still in regular use.

Bubble bum

Set out as many chairs as there are players, with a balloon on each chair. The players begin by sitting on the floor, with their legs crossed, a set distance away from the chairs. At your signal, they all rush to the chairs and have to sit on the balloons, trying to burst them.

As the balloons burst, they must rush back to their starting position and sit on the ground again, cross-legged. It's simple, but also great fun to play, if a little boisterous. To make the game rather trickier – and so make it last longer – don't blow the balloons up too much. A partially inflated balloon is far harder to burst!

Touchy feely

For this game, which has similarities to Twister, you need to hand a set of six stickers bearing the numbers from 1 to 6 to each of six players. Each person can choose where they'd like to stick the stickers about their person, be it on clothing or skin.

Everybody is assigned a number and the first person rolls a die to see who they are initially partnered with. If player one rolls a 5, for instance, followed by a 3, then he or she must touch player five's sticker number 3 with some part of their body and maintain contact throughout the rest of the game.

The next player similarly rolls the dice twice and ends up in contact with another sticker. It becomes progressively more tangled and difficult for players to keep in contact with the stickers, particularly if everyone starts laughing. Anyone who fails to keep contact should either be taken out of the game or made to perform some embarrassing forfeit.

Once all players have thrown the dice once and are attached to each other, put on some music and try to get them to dance. Parents of alarmingly advanced teenagers (is there any other kind?) may prefer to suggest this game only at parties with all girls or all boys.

Murder in the dark

Darkness and murder: two of children's favourite play topics, and a great game for parties, sleepovers and big gatherings. You need as many folded slips of paper as there are are players. All but two have 'Suspect' written on them. On the other two, one says 'Detective' and the other 'Murderer'.

The slips are either handed out in secret or are drawn from a bag. After removing anything that might hurt if it's bumped into (as well as the Ming Dynasty vase that you'd rather not have broken), the lights are turned off. The murderer must wander about the room touching people on the shoulder. All the Suspects he touches should fall to the ground with melodramatic, over-the-top dying noises. This goes on until the Murderer kills the Detective, at which point the Detective says, 'The Detective is Dead' and falls to the ground.

On go the lights with all the Suspects playing dead; if he or she chooses, the Murderer can play dead too. The Detective, however, is miraculously reincarnated and should go about the room studying the grisly carnage and trying to work out who they think the Murderer is. They must then make an accusation. If they get it right, they win. Get it wrong and the Murderer has won.

Wink murder

Although outwardly similar to *Murder in the dark*, there's a little more skill in this version. Slips of paper are drawn or distributed. All are blank except for one that bears the title of 'Murderer'.

Trying to avoid being spotted by anyone other than his victims, the Murderer should move about and wink at anyone he wants to 'kill'. Such deaths are usually again accompanied by hammy over-acting.

Accusations as to the Murderer can be made at any point by 'living' players but if somebody gets it wrong, they are immediately killed and out of the game. Some people insist on forfeits being paid as well to cut down on the number of accusations. Get the accusation right, though, and the game is won. The Murderer wins if only one other player is left living.

There are umpteen variants on this. One has a Detective leave the room while the rest of the group, in a circle, decide upon the Murderer. The Detective returns and stands in the middle of the circle as the Murderer begins felling victims with a wink while the Detective tries to guess who the Murderer is. Depending on the numbers playing, he is allowed up to three guesses.

Squeeze murder

Yet another murder game to be played with a decent-sized group in the dark. Players should be in a circle and pick pieces of paper from a hat, all of which are blank bar one bearing an 'M' for 'Murderer'.

When the lights do out, everybody holds hands. The murderer decides who he or she wants to murder, reckoning up how many places to their left that person is. The Murderer then squeezes the hand of the person to their left that number of times. That person should squeeze the hand of the person to their left one time fewer and so on until somebody feels their hand being squeezed only once. That person should die dramatically and move out of the circle.

There's no investigation here. It's just a bit of fun and continues until everyone is dead, unless of course the Murderer miscalculates and kills his or herself.

Bucket bounty

Rather than simply give children party bags stuffed with teeth-rotting sweets, tubs of bubbles and cheap knick-knacks, why not make them work for them? Set up several buckets – one might have sweets, the next a particular sort of toy, and so on.

Get the children to throw a tennis ball into the first bucket from a set distance. When they get the ball into the bucket, they can take their prize from it and pop it in their party bag. Those kids who don't succeed the first time can move a little nearer for their second go and nearer still if they don't get a prize that round. Once everyone has a prize from that bucket, you can move on to the second and so on. It helps them appreciate the party bags just that little bit more and has the added advantage that you don't have to stuff the bags yourself.

Party obstacle race

Set up an obstacle race, either timing how long it takes children to go round it or doubling it up with the obstacles in two lines, so that two teams can compete against each other. If there's a garden and the weather's decent, set it up outside.

Among the things you might think of including are:

- A coat to put on backwards

- Having to tie shoelaces or a tie with gloves on

- A row of chairs to crawl through

- A musical instrument on which a sound has to be made

- A skipping rope for a certain number of skips

- Food to eat without the use of hands

- A sheet of paper with a forfeit – sing the highest note you can, cluck like a hen, and so on

- A tarpaulin or sheet to crawl under

Plane madness

Hang on to your scrap paper for months before party time, particularly A4 paper you can't use in your printer. Sort everyone into two teams and set up something to

divide the room into two, either a line with a sheet thrown over it or a settee or table on its side.

Each team is given an equal number of sheets of paper and told to make them into darts. Once this is done, give them the signal and they must throw them, only one at a time, into the other team's part of the room, the aim being to see who has the fewest number of planes in their half when time is up. It's noisy but it's great fun, both to take part in and to watch.

Sofa samba

This is one of those rare party games that involves an element of strategy. It makes it marginally more difficult to begin with, but it's well worth it.

Two teams of four is the ideal number, and it's best if one team is all boys and the other all girls. The names of every player should be written on pieces of paper and handed out randomly, the idea being that everyone is not themselves, but the person on the piece of paper in their hand.

Group five chairs in a semi-circle in front of the sofa and have everyone sit down alternately, so there's a boy then a girl and so on, with four people on the sofa and one of the chairs unoccupied. The idea of the game is to get all of your team onto the sofa by getting the other team off it.

The game starts with whoever is sitting to the left of the empty chair. They call out somebody's name and the person with that name on the piece of paper must occupy the empty place, swapping their piece of paper with the person who has just called out. There's now a different empty space, so the person to the left of that should call out a name. Whoever holds it must sit in the empty place, swapping their paper with the caller.

As the game progresses, so the location of more names are steadily revealed. Players must keep track of where they are as they try to manoeuvre the other team off the sofa. The game ends when one team manages to get all their players onto it.

You can play with more people, if the couch will stand the strain, but the game takes correspondingly longer.

Knock knee shuffle

Two teams, two glasses or mugs or water a few yards away and two equal piles of loose change.

Players have to cram as many coins between their legs as possible, shuffle their way across to their glass and drop as many coins into it as they can, all of course without using their hands once the coins are in place. The team with the greater number of coins in the glass wins.

This is a variation on an old drinking game, which tended to involve the coins clenched somewhere a little less visible. The rules are the same, except that it was usually mandatory for the participants to hum the theme to *The Dambusters* while attempting to drop their bombs in the water.

Potato wars

Rather than throwing them out, keep hold of old pairs of tights and they'll come in very handy for party games. Put a couple of potatoes into one leg of the tights and tie the other leg around the player's waist, so that the tights hang down in front: put a balloon in front of each player.

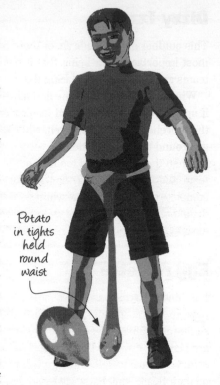

Potato in tights held round waist

The objective is to swing the 'bat', without using your hands in any way, so that it hits the potato forward. The game is a race between two people, either to get the potato to go a certain distance or to hit it into a goal of some sort. Potatoes or oranges work well on hard floors or out of doors but you might not want to risk using either on a beautiful shagpile carpet. You'd be better off substituting apples or ping pong balls.

This is a game that's every bit as entertaining to watch as to play, but if you're playing at a party, you can always turn it into a team game, the 'bat' being removed and tied round the next player's waist. If you have plenty of spare pairs of tights, make the players wear them on their heads and they'll look like old-style bank robbers.

The Malteser game

Pop some Maltesers in a bowl and get everyone sitting around it with a straw and a cup. A die gets passed around the circle, with each player rolling to see if they get a six. If not, it is passed to the next person. When somebody does roll a six, they try to get as many Maltesers as they can into their cup by sucking through the straw. They have until the next six is thrown.

It sounds easy, but gets very tricky if people begin laughing, for it then becomes well nigh impossible to keep the sweets on the end of the straw.

Dizzy Izzy

This outdoor game needs six or more people and two broomsticks or similar, the most important thing being that it has a smooth top. Divide everyone into two teams and line them up, placing the two sticks some distance away.

When the game begins, the first player in each team must run to the stick, place it upright with their forehead leaning on it and run around it ten times, keeping their forehead in contact with it, while the other players on the team count as they go around the stick ten times.

When they've finished ten laps of the stick, the players must run back to their team and tag the next person and so on, with the first team whose players all complete the task being the winners. What makes this so much fun is watching the drunkenly dizzy running as the players try to get back to their team. Even staying upright can be tricky.

Egg roulette

For obvious reasons, this is best played outside. If you do have to play it indoors, make sure you've got a tarpaulin or something similar covering the floor. Put as many eggs as there are players into a bowl. All are hard-boiled except for one.

Players have to select an egg from the bowl and hold them on their head. Somebody will be holding a raw egg, but nobody knows who. Each person is allowed to switch their egg once with another player.

When all the switches have been made, everyone must smash their egg against their forehead. Somebody is in for a nasty surprise. To keep the tension high, make them smash the eggs one by one.

Egghead aside: If you have another hard-boiled egg, you can demonstrate how to tell the difference between it and a raw egg without having to smash it open. Simply spin each of the eggs and lightly touch them as they are spinning, taking your finger off again quickly. Both eggs will stop spinning, but the raw egg will begin spinning again when you remove your finger. This is because, although the egg stopped moving, the yolk is still rotating inside the egg.

Another method is to spin them on their apexes. You can only manage this with hard-boiled eggs. To make the test more interesting, do it in a flat frying pan or on a tray with a thin layer of water. As the egg spins, water rises up the egg and starts spraying out like a lawn sprinkler.

Captain Freeze

At a party or other large gathering, one person should be appointed 'Captain Freeze'. Everybody else is told that if Captain Freeze freezes, suddenly being completely still, then everybody else should do the same.

Invariably there'll be one or two who take ages to notice that the room has gone suddenly quiet. The very last one to freeze becomes the new Captain Freeze. If you're playing at a party for youngish children, it makes sense for Captain Freeze only to go into his or her freeze routine at the instigation of an adult. Otherwise the guests are likely to spend the great part of their time motionless.

Hard taskmaster

Split the party up into groups of between four and six players. The Taskmaster calls out different tasks for the teams, who must carry them out as quickly as they can, the leader of a team shouting out 'Team ready for inspection, Taskmaster' when they believe they have completed a task.

At this point, the other teams must remain motionless and quiet, while the Taskmaster, possibly with the assistance of other onlookers, inspect the team to ensure that they have indeed carried out the task properly, giving them a point if they have. If not, the Taskmaster shouts out 'Task on' and the other teams then continue, with the first team penalised for jumping the gun by having to remain stationary.

Among the tasks that might be set are:

- arranging themselves in order of height, foot size or age

- swapping items of clothing

- taking off their shoes and putting them on their hands

- taking their jumpers off and putting them back on inside out

- putting the numbers 1 to 10 in alphabetical order

- pronouncing each of their names backwards with no mistakes

- sitting on the floor with their knees pressed against each other's backs

- eating a cream cracker each with no water

- peeling an apple each

4 Are we there yet?

WHEN WE WROTE *Dad Stuff*, we devoted a whole chapter to games you can play in the car to keep kids going on long journeys. All the games were tried and tested, and our kids loved them. But guess what? We've played those games so many times we've got bored with them. So here's a whole new set of car games – some traditional, some freshly minted – to keep the little darlings happy in the long gaps between motorway service stations.

The best games are those where Dad has to start things off and the kids can keep it going between them. You can join in too, of course, but if you're having trouble negotiating a busy roundabout in the pouring rain with a map balanced on your knees, while remembering that the French drive on the right, it can be tricky if that happens to be just the moment when everyone's waiting for you to remember the name of a country beginning with O. (There's only one, and it's Oman.)

The games in this chapter are both fun and, occasionally, educational – but you should never let on to your kids that you're secretly teaching them, when they think they're just having fun.

Faster! It's gaining on us!

Car snooker

Each player takes it in turn to be at the snooker table. Their turn begins when you pass a red car, equivalent to a red ball in snooker: they score one point. They then have to look out for the next snooker colour you pass, and score the value of that colour as if they'd potted that ball in snooker:

Yellow........ 2 points		Blue .... 5 points	
Green .... 3 points		Pink .... 6 points	
Brown........ 4 points		Black .... 7 points	

After spotting the colour, they then have to (s)pot another red car, then a colour again, and so on – just like snooker. If the first car you pass after a red car isn't one of the snooker colours, then it's the end of their break, and the next player gets to have a go.

To bring an added level of excitement into the game, you can introduce the idea of penalty points. If you pass a white car after the player's first red has been spotted, then this counts as potting the white ball; all the other players are awarded four points each, and the turn ends.

If you're the kind of Dad who likes to play strictly by the rules, then keep a tally of the number of red cars potted: once you've reached 15 (the number of red balls on a snooker table), then players have to pot each of the colours in turn. Y[ou'll be lucky to spot a pink car, though, unless Lady Penelope is driving past.

This is a game which works equally well on busy main roads and on motorways. If there's a lot of traffic, you can vary the rules to suit the circumstances: count only the cars that pass you in the opposite direction, for instance, or only the cars that you overtake.

Name that tune

Each player takes it in turn to hum the theme tune to a well-known film or TV show: whoever guesses it correctly has the next go.

This is a game that's harder for parents than it is for kids, as we'll constantly have to remember *not* to sing *Hawaii 5-0*, or *Magpie*, or any of a couple of dozen programmes our kids have never heard of but which are still rattling around in our heads thirty years after the damn shows stopped being broadcast.

Character counting

An excellent game, which we invented purely by chance. We were driving along, talking about what a great TV show *The Simpsons* is, and wondered how many regular characters there were. Thirty? Forty? We counted 130 in total – and that's just the characters who appeared enough times to be recognisable.

And so a game was born. Each player takes it in turn to name a character, with others helping out if they get stuck. The great thing is that this is a collaborative game, where you're all working together, rather than one in which you're pitched against each other. Leave it to the younger kids to come up with the obvious Marge, Homer, Mr Burns and so on, while more adept players nominate lesser-known characters such as Professor Frink and Principal Skinner's Mother.

It doesn't have to be just Simpsons, of course – choose the show that matches your family's viewing habits. Here's a suggestion of some character searches that should get you thinking:

Harry Potter (all books and movies)
Star Trek
Star Wars movies
Pantomimes
EastEnders/Coronation Street
The Beano
Premier League footballers
James Bond movies
Little Britain
Fairy stories
Nursery rhymes
Disney animations

Toy Story
Musicals
Lord of the Rings

As well as...
Politicians
Planets, stars and constellations
Artists and composers
TV presenters
Actors and actresses
Kings and queens
Cartoon animals

Countries of the world

The first player names a country beginning with A, such as Afghanistan. The next then has to think of a country that begins with the *last* letter of the country just named – Norway, for instance. And so the game continues, until no more countries can be thought of.

To make it easier, you can allow kids to think of cities as well; you may even choose to allow country names in their own language – Deutschland, España, and so on. And, of course, former names such as Ceylon and Rhodesia are allowed.

The number plate place game

Since the year 2001, all new cars have been issued with number plates that follow a standard format for displaying their place and date of origin:

AB52 CDE

The first letter shows the licence issuing centre, the second is a subcategory within that area. The next two numbers show the year and half year of registration: 02 is March to August 2002, and 52 is August 2002 to February 2003. The final three letters are randomly chosen, and identify individual cars.

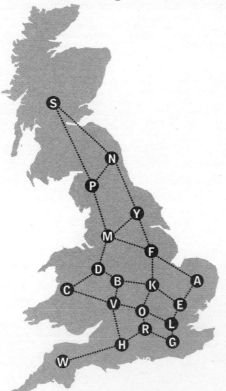

The map opposite shows the location of origin of all the current car plates. So a number plate that begins with A will have been sold in East Anglia, for instance. Most of the letters of the alphabet are used, with a few exceptions: I, J and Z are not used at all, and Q is used only for cars whose age cannot be verified (it may be an import or a kit car, for instance).

Simply spotting where the cars come from is entertaining in itself. But you can make a game of it by trying to get from one location to another – say from Cornwall to Scotland (that's W to S on the chart), only moving to the next location when you see a plate that's registered there. Follow the lines shown on the small map on the left to move from region to region.

This is the kind of game that can be played on busy motorways, and is a great ongoing game for long journeys: it's particularly satisfying if you happen to be driving from Cornwall to Scotland!

S
Scotland

N
Newcastle
& North

P
Preston
& Pennines

Y
Yorkshire

M
Manchester
& Merseyside

F
Forest & Fens

D
Deeside

B
Birmingham

K
Luton
& Northhants

A
East Anglia

C
Cymru

V
Vale of
Severn

O
Oxford

E
Essex & Herts

R
Reading

L
London

H
Hants & Dorset

G
Garden of England

W
West Country

Alphabet shopping

The first player begins, 'I went to the supermarket and I bought an apple.' The next player has to think of something you can buy in a supermarket beginning with B, such as bananas; the next player has to think of something beginning with C, and so on. (You'll be surprised how many people end up buying xylophones.)

Vary the game by visiting other kinds of shops – bookshops, record shops, and so on.

An alternative is for Dad to begin by saying, 'I went to a supermarket and bought something beginning with D.' All the kids then have to think of as many things you can buy in a supermarket that begin with that letter as they can. The advantage of this version is that Dad can choose easy or difficult letters, depending on the age of the children.

The name game

The first player says the name of a well-known figure, including a description of what they're well known for – such as 'Gordon Brown, politician'. The next player has to name someone who shares either the same first or second name: 'James Brown, singer'. And so it continues: 'Jesse James, outlaw'; 'Jesse Owens, athlete'; 'Michael Owen, footballer', and so on (you can take a few liberties with the names if you like). By specifying the characters' occupations, you're helping the kids to learn a little basic history – and proving that the person you've named is real.

A good variation is to miss out every other character, so that your kids have to work out the missing link. So if you go from 'Robbie Williams, singer' straight to 'Venus de Milo, statue', they have to figure out that the missing link is 'Venus Williams, tennis player.'

Celebrity challenge

This game is similar to Animal, Vegetable, Mineral, in that players have to ask questions to arrive at the solution. The difference is that in this game, you think of a well-known figure: your kids have to ask questions about their lives and accomplishments in order to work out who the person is.

Good questions include 'male or female', 'living or dead', 'real or imaginary' – since you can include cartoon and fictional characters as well. Liven things up by asking silly questions: 'Does he like mashed potato?', 'Has she got a hair dryer?', and so on. It's a game that makes kids think harder about celebrities, especially when it's their turn to think of someone: it's fun to see them struggling with such philosophical problems as whether or not Fred Flintstone owned a DVD player!

The noises game

This is a good game for younger players. Every time you pass something that makes a recognisable noise – a fire engine, a police car, a telephone box, a cow, a train, and so on – they have to make the noise of the object, and everyone else has to spot the thing they're emulating, and make the same noise when they see it.

Recommended only for Dads with strong nerves, particularly if they happen to be driving.

Uncle Bobby

Uncle Bobby reads books, but not magazines. He's a good accountant, although he can add, but he can't subtract. He eats noodles, but not pasta. He likes the colour green, but not blue or red.

Uncle Bobby, of course, only likes things that have double letters in them – and the clue is in his name. Once each player has worked out the rules, they can continue to take part by saying additional things that Uncle Bobby likes and dislikes.

The game can be adapted to incorporate other rules, just so long as they aren't too complicated to be guessed. So Mr Browning might only like things that contain 'ing' (skiing, but not football; sprinting, but not the high jump; swimming, but not golf; singers, but not musicians). You might include Aunt Jemima, who only likes things ending in a vowel; or Policeman Plod, who only likes two-word phrases in which both begin with the same letter.

What has an eye but no nose?

The answer, of course, is a needle. And it's a game that can be extended endlessly with little mental effort: you'd be surprised how many body parts are used figuratively in everyday speech.

Whoever's got it – give it back now

It doesn't have to be just body parts, of course: you could use pairs of objects associated with cars, for instance.

Here are some examples to get you started:

What has a tongue but no teeth? . . . . a shoe

What has teeth but no lips? . . . . a comb

What has legs but no arms? . . . . a table

What has arms but no hands? . . . . a coat (or a chair)

What has hands but no fingers? . . . . a clock

What has fingers but no knuckles? . . . . fish!

What has a neck but no head? . . . . a wine bottle

What has ears but no cheeks? . . . . corn

What has calves but no shins? . . . . a cow

What has brows but no lashes? . . . . a hill

What has shoulders but no arms? . . . . a motorway

What has a face but no hair? . . . . a watch

What has a beard but no moustache? . . . . a goat

What has palms but no wrists? . . . . a desert

What has feet but no knees? . . . . a tripod

What has skin but no fur? . . . . custard (or a drum)

What has canines but no molars? . . . . a dog's home

What has a heart but no liver? . . . . a lettuce

What has veins but no arteries? . . . . a leaf

What has a heel but no toes? . . . . a shoe

What has a chest but no shoulders? . . . . a pirate ship

What has three feet but no ankles? . . . . a yard

What has wings but no claws? . . . . a plane

What has feathers but no beak? . . . . a pillow

What has a horn but no teeth? . . . . a car

What has scales but no gills? . . . . a greengrocer

Scavenger hunt

Prepare a list of items to look out for on the journey, and print one out for each child. They cross each item off the list when they spot it. This is the kind of game that can be played, on and off, throughout a long trip.

If it's a route you know well, you can customise the list by adding things that you know you're going to pass on the way, but which may otherwise be rare. Here's a sample checklist you can photocopy:

☐ Church	☐ Tesco supermarket	☐ Ambulance
☐ Dog walker	☐ Phone box	☐ Tractor
☐ Statue	☐ Caravan	☐ Grain silo
☐ Road works	☐ Bus	☐ Electricity pylon
☐ Police car	☐ Taxi	☐ Plane overhead
☐ Boat	☐ Crane	☐ Post office
☐ Bridge	☐ Pig	☐ Foreign number plate
☐ School	☐ Vintage car	☐ 'School' sign
☐ Zebra crossing	☐ Shell petrol station	☐ 'Danger' sign
☐ Post box	☐ Man in uniform	☐ 'Old people' sign
☐ McDonald's	☐ Bus stop	☐ Horse box
☐ Little Chef	☐ GB sticker on car	☐ Flower seller
☐ Cow	☐ Train	☐ Traffic warden

If you don't mind your kids staring at other drivers, you can also add a list of things they might have with them, be wearing or be doing:

☐ Bluetooth headset	☐ Beard and glasses	☐ Picking their nose
☐ Moustache	☐ Tattoo on arm	☐ Talking on phone
☐ Three children	☐ Green jumper	☐ Sleeping passenger
☐ Dog in the car	☐ Sat nav	☐ Elderly couple
☐ Suit on hanger	☐ Eating	☐ Kids watching TV

Of course, the very best thing your kids can do while you're driving is to look out for speed cameras. Make sure they don't spot them out of the rear window, though. It'll be too late by then.

Car songs

Nothing helps revitalise sagging spirits on a long journey than a family sing-song. The most useful are those that continue for some time, either with variations of the words or with extensions to every verse.

Here are our favourite musical masterpieces. We've provided the music, too, just in case you happen to have a piano in your car.

On Top of Spaghetti

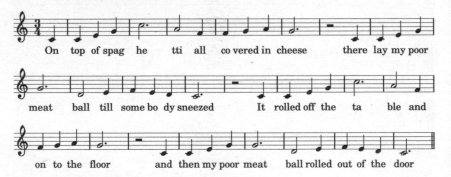

On top of spaghetti all covered in cheese.
I lost my poor meatball when somebody sneezed.

It rolled off the table, and onto the floor,
And then my poor meatball rolled out of the door.

It rolled in the garden and under a bush,
And then my poor meatball was nothing but mush.

The mush was as tasty as tasty could be,
And early next year it grew into a tree.

The tree was all covered with beautiful moss.
It grew great big meatballs and tomato sauce.

So if you eat spaghetti all covered with cheese,
Hold on to your meatball and don't ever sneeze.

Johnny was a Paratrooper

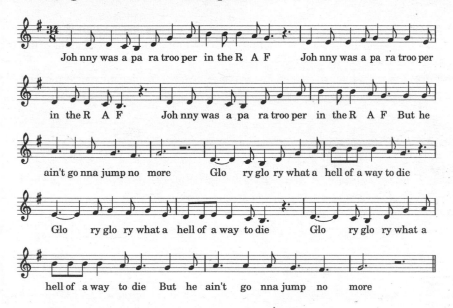

Johnny was a paratrooper in the RAF, Johnny was a paratrooper in the RAF
Johnny was a paratrooper in the RAF, But he ain't gonna jump no more.

Glory, glory, what a hell of a way to die, Glory, glory, what a hell of a way to die
Glory, Glory, what a hell of a way to die, But he ain't gonna jump no more.

He jumped without a parachute from 40,000 feet...

They scraped him off the tarmac like a blob of raspberry jam...

They put him in an envelope and sent him home to mum...

She put him on the mantelpiece for everyone to see...

She put him on the table when the vicar came to tea...

The vicar spread him on his toast and said, 'What lovely jam'...

You'll Never Get to Heaven

The trouble with many songs is remembering the lyrics. This one gets around the problem by getting Dad to say the lines first, which are then repeated by everyone else.

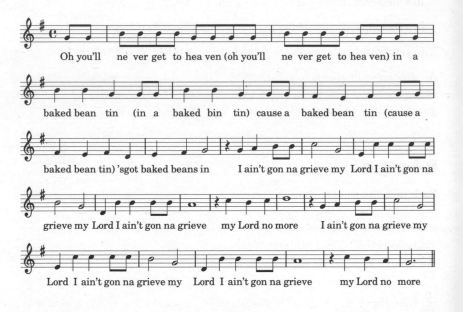

Oh, you'll never get to heaven in a baked bean tin
Cause a baked bean tin's got baked beans in.

I ain't gonna grieve my Lord, I ain't gonna grieve my Lord
I ain't gonna grieve my Lord no more
I ain't gonna grieve my Lord. I ain't gonna grieve my Lord
I ain't gonna grieve my Lord no more

…On a furry mat, cause the Lord will think you killed his cat

…On a jumbo jet, cause the Lord ain't built no runways yet

…In a bottle of gin, cause the Lord won't let no spirits in

…On rollerskates, cause you'll roll right past those pearly gates

...On a boy scout's knee, cause a boy scout's knee is knobbly

...In an old Ford car, cause an old Ford car won't get that far

...In a ping pong ball, cause a ping pong ball is much too small

...In a limousine, cause the Lord ain't got no gasoline

...In a rocking chair, cause the Lord don't want no rockers there

...In your girlfriend's bra, cause your girlfriend's bra don't stretch that far.

An alternative chorus is to substitute the following for the third and fourth lines of the chorus at a faster speed: 'I ain't gonna drink, I ain't gonna swear, I ain't gonna...Ooh, I wouldn't dare', and then on to the last line as before.

B-i-n-g-o

Each time the song is sung, it changes slightly: first one and then successively more of the letters of the name are clapped instead of sung. The second time around, for example, the spelling part would be 'clap-I-N-G-O'; the third time, it's 'clap-clap-N-G-O'. The sixth and final time the song is sung, all five letters are clapped.

There was a far mer had a dog and Bin go was his name o   B   I   N G O

B   I   N G O   B   I   N G O and Bin go was his name o

There was a farmer had a dog
and Bingo was his name-o
B-I-N-G-O, B-I-N-G-O, B-I-N-G-O,
and Bingo was his name-o.

If you're driving, perhaps you shouldn't take both hands off the steering wheel to clap, particularly if you're driving past a police car at the time.

Worms

A very silly song indeed.

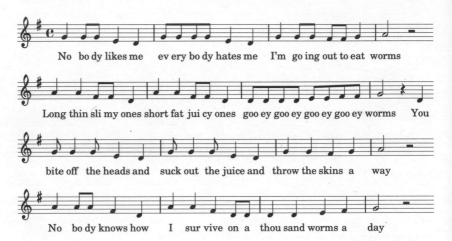

Nobody likes me
Everybody hates me
I'm going out to eat worms
Long thin slimy ones,
Short fat juicy ones
Gooey, gooey, gooey, gooey worms.

You bite off the heads,
And suck out the juice,
And throw the skins away
Nobody knows how I survive
On a thousand worms a day!

Long thin skinny ones
Slip down easily,
Big fat juicy ones stick.
Hold your head back
Squeeze their tail
And their juice just goes drip, drip.

Have you any idea where I've been?

5 Surf and turf

THERE'S NOTHING SIMON LIKES BETTER than spending a day frolicking on the beach, splashing about in the waves and building sandcastles... or at least lying down watching the kids doing it. For Steve, on the other hand, the beach is seen as the holiday setting from hell: not enough shade, too many over-oiled bodies, nowhere comfortable to sit, and the rest of the evening spent scraping sand out of every orifice.

For those who *do* like to be beside (tiddley-om-pom-pom), here's a collection of games and pastimes, as well as a handy guide to the seashells you might find.

For those who prefer the security of feeling the grass beneath their feet, we've a range of outdoor activities – as well as a guide to how to stay afloat (and ensure that your kids do too) while messing about in boats.

If your love of the Great Outdoors extends to sleeping out under the stars, we've a few ideas for turning a camp fire into a meal to remember (and we're not talking about food poisoning here).

What is sand?

Q: Why is it impossible to be hungry on the beach?
A: Because of all the sand which is there.

It's often difficult for young minds to get their head around the fact that sand is made of tiny pieces of rock which have been weathered over the millennia and washed down rivers or blown into the sea where, along with shell, it's ground up further as currents and waves move it about. The rounder a bit of sand or pebble is, the further it has probably travelled.

Although not all 'beaches' are sandy, those that are have the lighter, sandy bits on top while the bigger bits of rock have sunk lower down. There are people – known as psammophiles – who collect sand. This doesn't usually mean bringing lots of it back from a day trip to Mablethorpe, but finding sand of varying colours, textures and so on. In Hawaii, for instance, there are black, green and red sands.

Sand collectors and others use the 'Wentworth Article Size Classification' under which anything between 0.06mm and 2mm is defined as sand. Anything over 2mm is known as gravel, including granules, pebbles and cobbles, while anything over 256mm is a boulder. Particles below 0.06mm are known as silt – finer than sand but still gritty. Below 0.0004mm is clay or mud, the finest material of all, which will feel smooth if you rub it on your teeth and, if it gets wet, becomes a sticky ball.

What is quicksand?

It's a mixture of sand and salty water and is actually a liquid, which is why objects that are thrown in have a tendency to sink. Despite the cinematic cliché of quicksand sucking people to their death, it's actually denser than water so that, unless you're wearing heavy equipment, you'll probably float.

Quicksand is often found under leaves and crusts of mud, or near limestone caves where underground springs reach the surface. If you do fall into quicksand, stay calm. Often it won't come any higher than your knees or waist. Even if it is deeper, most people will float once once they're waist-deep. The problems comes if you wriggle about, because that will pull you down further. With a consistency like treacle, however, it is hard to get out of quicksand.

Keep calm, get rid of anything heavy like a rucksack and try to float on your back. Eventually, your legs and feet should come back up to the surface. Make small circular motions with your legs, which will help keep the quicksand at the surface watery, and slowly paddle your way towards more solid ground.

Nekki

This Japanese children's game simply requires the players to try to knock down a stick stuck in the sand with other sticks. You need a reasonably long and stout stick pushed into the sand as the target, or you could use one of those bamboo canes with a fishing net on the end.

You need to find as many smaller but similar sticks to throw at it as there are players. Mark the throwing positions in the sand, handicapping the stronger players by making them throw from further away. The first to knock over the target is the winner of that round.

Beach darts

Draw a series of concentric circles in the sand, assigning increasing points to them the closer they are to the centre.
Each player should be sent off to find three similar objects they can throw, such as pebbles or a particular type of shell.

Throw the objects in turn, adding up the score after each round and keeping track by writing in the sand.

Lame Hen

This is a relay race for a sizeable number of people that apparently originates in China, though you could just as easily pretend to your warlike offspring that it's an obstacle course game played by the army. Get them to gather up twenty sticks, which ought to be at least six inches long – ideally double that.

Line them up in two rows about 40cm apart, rather like rungs on a ladder. Organise the players into two equal teams some distance away from the sticks. The first person in each team should hop on one leg over all the sticks, pick the last one, then return to the beginning, putting the stick down so it becomes the new first stick in the 'ladder'.

This is the signal for the next person to set off. The first team to complete the course once wins. If children are too small to hop on one leg, they can always do the bunny hop instead. The Chinese apparently require the hoppers to cluck like hens. We found a marked reluctance on the part of our guinea pigs to do this, on the grounds that it was 'so not cool'.

Boules

If you haven't a Kubb set to hand (see *Dad Stuff* p.148), Boules is the next best game to take to the beach. A set consists of a small jack and eight metal or weighted plastic balls with markings identifying them as pairs. The French take the game very seriously: they call the game Pétanque, and it's boules that they throw. They play on hard terrain like dirt or gravel rather than on the beach. The great advantage of playing on the beach is that you can always run into the sea to cover your annoyance at having been beaten by your children.

Play with two teams of one or two players on each side. You can choose whether to play with two or four boules. With four people, it's two boules each. Don't play in sand that's too soft, or the boules will simply stop where they land, making it a much less skilful game.

Although there are no rules about how boules should be thrown, it's usual to hold the ball in the hand, palm downwards. This way, backspin can be imparted to the boule in an attempt to get it to stop where it lands, rather than overshooting the jack, rolling down the hill and ending up in the sea.

The person who begins draws a line in the sand with their foot and, standing behind it, throws the jack. They should then try to get a boule as close to the jack as possible. Touching it is fine. A player from the second team should try to get

You all right, Jack?

a boule closer to the jack than the first team, if necessary knocking their boule out of the way. Play continues with the team furthest from the jack throwing next. After every player has thrown, points are scored for all the boules a team has that are nearest the jack. If, for instance, a team has three boules closer to the jack than any of the other team, they score three points. The first to 13 points is usually the winner of that game, but you can set any total you wish.

How to determine which ball is nearest the jack

We still remember arguments over boules from childhood family holidays over boules, with hankies brought out to measure the distance of two competing balls from the jack. While amusing as a spectator sport, no two hankies seemed to tell the same story and, these days, who has a hankie handy anyway, particularly if you're wearing swimming trunks?

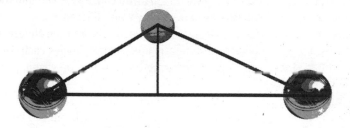

Fortunately, there's a much easier way of determining which boule is closest to the jack. Imagine a triangle formed by the two boules and the jack. Stand behind the jack and visualise a line drawn to meet, at right angles, a line drawn between the two boules. Whichever boule is nearest to that meeting point is the one closest to the jack.

Beach bowling

Damp sand's the perfect stuff for setting up your own bowling alley on the beach. Depending on what sort of ball you plan on using, fill either a bucket or a plastic cup with sand and upend it to make ten 'pins'. Arrange them in a triangle with one in the front row, then two, then three, then four.

A pin is scored not when it is hit, but when no flat surface remains on the top. It's a mite tedious having to reset the pins so either set up two or three lanes to start with or else place two sets of pins opposite each other and have two teams, rolling in turn to see who can demolish all ten pins first. Depending on the skill of the players and the solidity of the ball you're playing with, you might want to give each player two rolls of the ball at a time, rather than just the one.

If you're at Southport and the sea's too far away to dampen the sand, or you want to play when you aren't at the beach, empty plastic water bottles or drinks cans can also be pressed into service as pins.

Castles in the sand

Children find making things from sand well nigh irresistible but they often need a helping hand. That's *our* excuse, at any rate.

It's a great deal easier building castles and other sculptures if you give it some thought before you set off. Making anything substantial with the sort of plastic spade you get at most seaside resorts is hard going. If you're travelling by car, take a garden spade or, even better, a shovel. Yes, it looks completely over the top when you arrive on the beach in the morning. But the sneering of other parents will change to envy when they realise just how quickly you can get the job done and return to reading your suntan-cream-and-sand-covered paperback while watching them struggle to build a castle half the size of yours.

Planning and tools: Have a good hunt round before you set off for things that could be useful. Plastic implements and shapes of the sort bought for young children can be handy, along with old pastry knives, trowels, rulers, plastic containers, skewers, paintbrushes and straws (great for getting rid of loose sand) as well as an assortment of cutlery of the type that tends to lurk at the bottom of drawers. You can actually *buy* sand-sculpting tools, but then you have no excuse if it looks any less than brilliant.

If you intend making anything substantial then you need sand that is good and wet. Not all beaches lend themselves to this, but if you can site your construction area around the high-water mark and dig down to water, that's ideal. With the spade or shovel you so sensibly brought with you, mix the sand and water up really well before you begin. Start it too near the sea and you risk having the sea wipe out all your hard work before it's finished.

Starting to build: The traditional dad and children castle seems to involve plonking a big mound in the middle, making a few turrets using upside-down buckets and then shaping some walls. By all means use the sand you've dug out of the hole as a base, but you can make the construction more impressive by building a tower or two to begin with.

If you can find something to make a cylindrical mould, splendid. Fill the shape with sand, packing it down as you go. If not, then link your hands and scoop out as much sand from the hole as you can, plonking the 'pancake' on top of the mound, holding it while the water drains from it. This will bond the layers of sand and is the secret to making a sandcastle that lasts. Keep on piling 'pancakes' of sand on top, each smaller than the one underneath so the tower doesn't get too top heavy.

Simon hard at work (out of shot) watching his friend Peter build a sandcastle

Making walls: For walls connecting the towers or around a central tower, you need to get the sand into 'brick' shapes, holding your hands parallel and a few inches apart, again letting the water drain. Do one layer of bricks at a time, trying to make them a regular size, then do the same on the next level and so on. The kids could start carving the towers while you are doing this, giving the towers pointy tops, carving recesses for windows and doors, adding balconies and stairs, etching the outline of stones and so on. This is where all those tools you brought with you really come into their own.

The walls will almost certainly need to be castellated, preferably with a walkway in the middle for the troops (no matter where you are in the world, the supermarket is almost certain to sell packs of plastic soldiers to add to your castle). Staircases

Who needs to go to Jordan to see the temple at Petra?

are best made by constructing a ramp and then cutting out the steps. If you're brave enough, try for an arch or two. You can carve away at a wall to create a hole that you shape into an arch. Alternatively, for a truly impressive arch, build two towers close together, bringing them near each other at the top and have someone hold their hand to support sand as you create a bridge between them.

Extra decoration and twiddly bits can be added by getting extremely wet sand and letting it dribble out of your hand where you need it. If the sand is getting dry in places, a spray bottle will restore the sand to a state where you can work with it again.

We have a fondness for building roads that descend into tunnels under our castles. Sometimes they go all the way through and out the other side, but they don't have to. If you've timed it well, now could be a good time to construct a moat, ready to receive the tide as it comes back in.

Bear in mind that most beach sand is nothing like the quality of sand used by those amazing sand sculptors. So don't feel too inadequate if your effort ends up looking more like a ruined burial mound than the Taj Mahal. And if you finish with a flourish, only to discover that the children vanished over an hour earlier, you might have been taking it all a little too seriously.

Sand boats and other creatures

The more impressive a sandcastle is, the less suitable it will be for the kids to play in. They tend to love holes, of course, and it's very easy to oblige if you've brought a decent spade or shovel with you. Don't get carried away, though, by making it too deep. If the sides collapse, it could be dangerous. Don't forget that when the hole no longer seems exciting to them, you can get them to stand in it and bury them up to their waists, packing the sand down so it takes them ages to wriggle their way out.

The other standby is the sand boat, almost invariably something resembling the sort of craft you get on a park lake. You don't need to be quite as particular over the wetness of the sand as you would for a large-scale castle. Build it with a pointy end and a couple of raised seats inside. Use shells for the dials on the dashboard, perhaps using an inverted bucket or frisbee for the steering wheel. A car is only a little more adventurous. Model two-thirds of the wheels against the body, tie sticks together to make a Flintstone-like roof and make use of driftwood, shells, seaweed and the like for decoration, indicators, lights, number plate and so on.

If you're of an artistic bent, then don't stick to man-made objects. Umpteen creatures can be conjured up out of sand, be they dragons, dinosaurs, hippos or snakes.

Sea shells

What visit to the seaside would be complete without returning with a handful of shells? We used to put them in airtight jars, only to watch the water turn green over time. The longer they were left, the more odious was the odour when the water was eventually thrown away. But what *are* the shells we see all the time on the beach? In the absence of an informative 'she' selling seashells by the seashore, here's a guide to some of the more common ones and an explanation of how to tell the age of a shell.

Scallop

The scallop is a bivalve – its shell is in two halves – and was used as the design for the Shell logo. Although the shells are often washed up on beaches, the scallop lives in deep water where predators are fewer. It can actually swim, which it does fairly nippily by opening and shutting its shell, forcing water out on either side of the hinge. They are hermaphrodites, having both male and female sex organs. Scallops are edible. The great scallop, which can be as much as six inches across, often ends up as an ashtray.

Mussel

The mussel is another bivalve. Very tough, it attaches itself to rocks, jetties, piers and the like. Purple or dark blue on the outside, the two halves of the shell are held together by a powerful adductor muscle. They get their food by filtering water but should only be eaten when properly cultivated – usually on ropes – in areas where the cleanliness of the water is guaranteed. If you find a mussel shell with a little round hole drilled in it, this will be from a dog whelk which bores into a mussel then sucks it out!

I've lived here since I was a young shaver

Periwinkle

Common throughout the UK, the best-known periwinkle is the edible variety which can be as much as 5cm long. The conical shells have a spiral ridge though this becomes less pronounced in older winkles. The periwinkle is a gastropod, the marine equivalent of a snail or slug. All gastropods have one large 'foot' for moving around.

Razor shells

The long, thin, discarded shells aren't uncommon, though finding one with both sides in perfect condition, still joined, is rarer. Few of us have actually seen the creatures themselves. Living vertically in sand, they shy away from light and vibration, and can burrow down faster than somebody could dig with a spade.

Limpet

The conical protective shell of the common limpet, one of several limpet varieties in the UK, has probably been taken home in more buckets than any other. Limpets can live for fifteen years. They use their tough watertight seal to cling tenaciously to rocks, feeding off algae by moving slowly and scraping at it with a sort of conveyor belt of teeth. Don't try to prise a live limpet off its rock or you could kill it.

Cockle

This thick, rounded, ridged shell is a bivalve, although it's rare to find both halves still joined. Cockles live in shallow burrows which are often exposed after storms. Like most bivalves they don't grow much in winter, so you can tell its age by looking at the number of bands running across the ridges. The dark lines are the winter marks, the lighter bands are where growth has speeded up in the warmer weather.

Messing about in boats

It may be that the smallest boat you've been in since you were a kid is a cross-Channel ferry yet, for some reason, every Dad is supposed to know how to mess about on the water. You may be lucky and find that the only transportation for hire is a pedalo. But if you're being badgered to take your children out in a rowing boat, a punt or a canoe, you'd better have some idea of what to do. Whatever method of transport you end up with, make sure they're wearing flotation devices, even if they are decent swimmers.

Rowing

We aren't talking about trying to get into the Oxford and Cambridge Annual Boat Race here, just being able to handle a rowing boat for a fun trip on a river or lake without making yourself look too ridiculous. It's a good idea to know that the pointy end is the front or bow and that you have to sit with your back to it.

Before you start: Make sure that the oars provided are of the same length, with paddles at the end that are the same size as each other and undamaged. The oars should be roughly double the width of the boat and you should also check that the rowlocks, the circular pivots the oars fit in, are in decent condition and pivot freely. The oars must also have a stop to prevent them slipping through the rowlocks. If anything is amiss, sort it out there and then or you will have a miserable time, made worse when your attempts to shift the blame are not believed.

Technique: Remember that you face away from the direction you're going. Fit the oars in the rowlocks with the full face of the blades facing the stern of the boat. Sitting as comfortably as you are able and with the oar blades out of the water, stretch forwards as far as you can. Dip the blades in the water and pull back, using your weight to help get the oars through the water. If there's something to brace your legs against, so much the better.

Use your legs, then your back and finally your arms to pull. At the end of the stroke, lift the oars so the blades are slightly out of the water, stretching forwards to repeat over again. And over again. And again. Find a stroke that is comfortable over a long period rather than trying to go too fast from the word go – you may be in for the long haul.

It's important to pull with the blades just under the surface of the water so you need to experiment to get the pitch of the blades right. If the angle is too far back, the blades will pull themselves too far under. If it's too far forward, the oars will skip along the surface and you may fall backwards. As you become more confident, you can turn your hands back a little for the return stroke so the oars are 'feathered' and offer less wind resistance.

Steering: To make small changes in direction, pull one oar less strongly than the other. If you need to adjust your heading more drastically, lift one oar clear of the water while still pulling with the other. Some rowing boats have tillers which

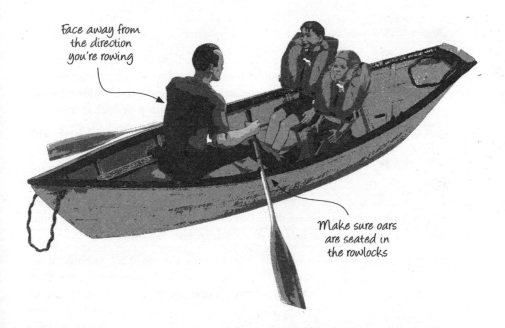

Face away from the direction you're rowing

Make sure oars are seated in the rowlocks

makes the rower's job easier, unless the child assigned to tiller duty decides that their favourite way of progressing up the river is in zig-zags. You should probably look behind you from time to time, just in case they think it would be fun to ram another boat.

If you need to change positions at any time, keep as low and near the centre of the boat as you can.

If you row for any length of time and it's not something you're used to, be prepared for some sizeable blisters and aching muscles the next day.

Canoeing

There are essentially two types of canoe. The enclosed kayak type that originated with the Eskimos have double-bladed paddles and are certainly nippy but are generally just for one person. More suitable for family outings is the open, more stable Canadian canoe. They use paddles with only one blade and Dad is usually positioned in the back doing most of the work.

Even if there is somebody in front paddling, it's important to know how to control the canoe on your own as the enthusiasm of your co-paddler may diminish after a while. Sit up as straight as you can (sometimes kneeling is more comfortable). For paddling on the left, hold the top of the paddle with your right hand and have your left much lower down. The paddle should go into the water almost vertically with the blade at 90 degrees to the direction of the canoe.

The J-stroke: If you simply pull the paddle back, you will start heading to the right. So your action must end in a 'J-stroke'. As you near the end of the stroke, use your top hand to twist the paddle 90 degrees so that it's parallel to the canoe and push the blade of the paddle away from the boat a little (from above the whole stroke looks vaguely like the letter 'J'). In this way, the paddle also acts as a rudder turning the canoe back to the left and keeps you on track. The more you push away from the canoe, the more you will turn. For paddling on the right, switch the hands over to the other side of the canoe and carry out a mirror image stroke.

The J-stroke pushes the rear of the canoe away from the paddle. You should also know the 'draw stroke' which pulls the canoe towards the paddle (and thus helps you head to the right if you're paddling on the left). Stretch out to the side with the blade parallel to the canoe and pull in the paddle, largely using your bottom hand. As the blade nears the canoe turn the paddle and continue the stroke, pushing the blade backwards and keeping the canoe going forwards.

The sweep stroke: For tight steering, you can use the 'sweep stroke'. The paddle is held out to the side with the bottom hand further up the shaft and the blade in the normal orientation. Putting the blade only partly in the water, bring the paddle in an arc towards the rear of the canoe. As the blade isn't fully in the water, it's easy to do several sweep strokes quickly. It will bring the rear of the canoe to the side you're paddling, but you'll get little foward movement.

Don't hold the paddle too tightly for any of the canoe strokes. A slightly loose grip will actually help to keep control and, even more importantly, minimise the aches and pains that are almost certain to come.

Kneeling
may be more
comfortable
than sitting

Give the paddle a twist
at the end for a J-stroke

Two people paddling: When you're canoeing with somebody in front, you must emphasise that the person in the rear is in charge. You should generally paddle on opposite sides of the canoe with the rear canoeist calling out when they want to switch paddles from one side to the other. For much of the time, the person in the front will simply be providing forward motion by pulling their paddle back in the water, lifting it and repeating it ad nauseum. Very minor changes of direction can be accomplished by the rear person making a stronger or weaker stroke.

As with rowing, it's much more satisfying and efficient to use regular, moderate strokes rather than going hell for leather and finding that you're exhausted a mile away from where you started. If want to teach the person in the front something other than the basic pull, the draw stroke is probably the most useful. This way, you can turn the canoe quickly in case you have to avoid trees, other boats or prehistoric monsters.

Kayaks are usually enclosed and generally, though not always, made for single person use. However, in order to be able to use one safely, it is essential that you know how to roll it and escape from it if it capsizes, something far better taught by a qualified instructor.

Punting

It's a sunny day, you're in Oxford or Cambridge and the bright young things are drifting past effortlessly in lovely flat-bottomed punts. What could be more fun than a family outing on a punt? Be warned. Of all the forms of messing about on water, none offer quite so comprehensive a chance for the novice to look a complete fool – and possibly end up with a ducking.

Although you can rent punts on the Avon, the Thames and elsewhere, the two places most closely associated with punting are the Cherwell and Isis in Oxford, and the Cam in Cambridge. Naturally, Oxford and Cambridge do things differently.

The Cambridge technique: stand at the back of the boat and try not to fall in

Which university was it Daddy didn't go to, Oxford or Cambridge?

The Cambridge technique: Punt from the deck at the back (the 'till'), standing sideways on and a little nearer the side you want to punt on. The pole should be raised, hand over hand, until it is clear of the water. The aim is to have it vertical as you look from back to front, but angled back a little as you'd see it from the side, so that you are able to push with it, though, once the punt is moving, it can be completely vertical.

Open your hands and let the pole drop to the river bed, keeping your hands around it. Grip and push the pole along the bottom, letting your hands 'walk' up the pole as the punt moves forwards. At the end of the stroke, when your hands are near the top of the pole, grip it again, giving it a twist just in case it is stuck in mud. The pole will probably be around 30 degrees from the vertical at this point. The pole, these days usually made of metal, should float behind the boat. At this point, as the punt glides along, the pole becomes a rudder. Pivoting your body, move the pole gently to the left to turn left and to the right to turn right. Then, when you're ready, begin pulling the pole up, hand over hand, getting it ever more vertical until it clears the water and you're ready to let go again.

The Oxford technique: At Oxford and pretty much everywhere else but Cambridge, people punt from inside the boat which, Cambridge people claim, leads to more splashing of the occupants. They also use the punts the other way around, with the till at the front, but you'll be told about this when you hire it.

Whichever punting method you use, it is very important not to get carried away and run out of pole. Don't leave it till the last inch or two before gripping or this will be the moment that the pole gets stuck in mud and either drags you into the water with it or leaves the punt moving forward with the pole still sticking out of the water and receding into the distance. The punt will be provided with a paddle, but having to go back for the pole is likely to invite ribald comment, and not only from your own family. If the bottom is muddy, don't push down vertically with the pole but angle it further backwards, even though it might mean you don't move as quickly.

Resist the temptation to move about as you punt or you may find yourself walking back too far and end up clinging to the pole as the punt continues on. Trying to get past other punts by heading under trees with hidden low branches can also lead to disaster, as Simon can testify, having been knocked off this way recently. Naturally, he claims this was essential research to see how easy it is to climb back into a punt (very easy). Just as naturally, nobody believes him.

I knew I should have left my phone in the car

Touch football, American style

Despite several attempts to get to grips with the rules of American football on trips to the USA, it remains mystifying, though we had no trouble mastering 'tailgating' which essentially entails having boozy, pre-game picnics at college games using the back of a pickup truck as a table.

However, we've had great family fun playing this slimmed down version, which has some of the exhilaration of British Bulldog though it's probably well-nigh unrecognisable to connoisseurs of the game proper. Those bruising tackles that make rugby seem a game for softies are replaced by a simple one or two-handed touch below the neck. A variant on this is to stuff long socks, scarves or similar into pockets or waistbands and have 'tackling' players grab these instead.

You need a reasonable-sized playing area with two end zones, much like rugby. The ball doesn't have to be oval shaped, although this is better. You need at least three players on each team. Only one team is attacking at any time; the other is defending. The best thrower on the attacking team is chosen as quarterback.

Play begins with a 'scrimmage', in which one player stands at the midpoint of the pitch and passes the ball backwards between their legs to the quarterback. The quarterback has four seconds free of being tackled to throw the ball to one of their team anywhere on the pitch. The aim of this person, the 'receiver', is to run with the ball into the opposition's end zone without being tackled. The ball can only be transferred once in each 'play'.

The quarterback may choose to run with the ball, but if they do they can be tackled and can't throw it to another player. If the player with the ball is touched, play stops and there's another scrimmage. The centre again passes the ball between their legs to the quarterback for another play.

The attackers have four goes to get the ball into the opposing end zone. This counts as a touchdown (though the player doesn't actually have to place the ball on the ground) and scores six points. If the ball goes out of bounds or touches the ground, that play ends and the ball is returned to the site of the previous scrimmage for the next play.

Goal! After a touchdown, two of the defenders form goalposts, holding hands horizontally, while their free arms point upwards. An attacker throws the ball backwards to another player who puts it down for a third person to try to kick

Kick the ball too close to a goalpost and it's likely to run away

it between the posts and over the bar. Despite the difficulty of converting, it only scores one point.

Following the conversion attempt, the attackers return to their endzone and kick the ball upfield for the other team who grab it and now become the attackers. Until they touch the ball, however, it is not in play and the new defenders can't touch it.

From the spot where attackers are first tackled, they begin their four attempts at a touchdown with their first scrimmage. If the attackers fail to score a touchdown with their four plays, play switches direction, with the opposition becoming the attackers at the point where the last tackle was made.

Now they have four plays for a touchdown. If at any point a defender gets hold of the ball in the air or on the ground, their team now has possession and they become the attackers with the first of their four scrimmages starting at that point.

And so it goes on, until everyone is exhausted or a prearranged total is reached. In the real game, there's a good deal of strategy and, without taking so long that the opposing team get bored and look for something else to do, it can be fun to try to devise team gameplans before each play, even if they almost never pan out.

Frisbee® golf

We're not allowed to mention Frisbees® without using that annoying ®, which frankly is a bit of a pain in the ®s. So we're going to call them discs instead, but you know what we're referring to, right?

If you get bored of throwing the disc to and fro, here's a great variation which lends itself well to a beach or a park. If you aren't playing solo, you'll need a disc for each player. First, decide on a course of whatever size you choose. You might assign a tree as the first 'hole'; a deckchair as the second; a lamp post as the third, and so on. As with golf, players have to hit the tree with as few throws as possible, taking each successive throw from the point where the previous one landed. Players compete for that hole and then move on to others.

To our surprise, we learned that there is a Professional Disc Golf Association

which holds world championships. Not only that, it seems that many American parks have disc golf courses, with metal baskets as each 'hole'. There are even special discs for the game, divided into drivers, mid-range and putters.

Given our ability to throw the things unintentionally into the middle of people picnicking fifty yards to one side of us, we'll stick to the simple version.

Kingo

Kingo was one of Simon's favourite games at primary school – that and running up and down the school playground pretending to be a police car and singing the theme tune to *Z-Cars*.

The game, best with a large group, begins with all the players standing in a circle with their legs apart and their feet touching the next person. Somebody bounces a tennis ball in the middle, calling out the letters of 'Kingo', one per bounce, letting it drop to the ground after the last. It will inevitably roll towards one of the players, who have to kick the ball away to someone else if they can, pivoting on their toes like the flippers on a pinball machine.

The player whose legs the ball eventually goes through becomes 'It'. Everyone runs away within the designated playing area and when 'It' grabs the ball, they yell out 'Stop' and all the other players must halt and stay stationary. Depending on the size of the area being played in, 'It' either throws the ball at any other player from there or takes one stride for each letter of 'Kingo', calling out each letter as they go, and then throws the ball, aiming at the legs.

The player hit then becomes 'It' and round and about you go. One variant has the hit players joining 'It' and throwing the ball between them preparatory to nailing a player.

Forfeit catch

Any number of players group themselves in a circle, giving themselves plenty of room. The ball – a tennis ball is ideal – is thrown randomly to other players. Anyone dropping the ball has to work their way through a series of forfeits.

First drop: one hand behind their back.

Second drop: stand on one leg, still keeping their hand behind their back.

Third drop: go down on one knee.

Fourth drop: go down on both knees.

Fifth drop: close one eye.

Sixth drop: out of the game.

If, however, they catch the ball after receiving a forfeit, they progress back through the forfeits, one step at a time.

So somebody down on one knee who catches the ball can now stand, though it must be on one leg. Catch it again and they can stand on both feet, but still with their hand behind their back.

Of course, there's some skill required to throw the ball to another player – especially if the one throwing is on their knees with one eye shut and an arm behind their back. You should be judicious in choosing when to allow the ball to be re-thrown if a catch seems to be impossible.

Raising cane

If you have a bamboo cane lying about that is six feet long or so, here's an activity that will mystify children and – to be honest – us too, until we figured out what was going on.

You need four or more children standing side by side. Hold the cane so that it's balancing on your two outstretched middle fingers, and tell them that you want them, as a team, to lower the stick to the ground, doing so yourself as you explain it.

Have the kids put their arms out with their middle fingers extended (those that can't manage this are allowed to use their index fingers). When they're all roughly in line, lay the cane on their fingers and tell them to lower it to the floor, *without any of them letting the cane slip off their fingers.*

Bizarrely, instead of going down, the cane will invariably rise upwards instead: they'll be so anxious to maintain finger contact with the cane that they'll tend to push it up rather than risk it falling off.

You can always dress this up as a magic trick. As you command them to try to lower it, stare with wide eyes, mutter some mumbo-jumbo and lift your arms, palms upwards, as if commanding the stick to rise. Be warned, though, that the 'magic' will quickly fade as they do work out how to lower it, so don't do it more than once or twice.

If you have two canes and eight children or more to hand, arrange them so they're facing each other in two lines and turn it into a competition to see who can lower their cane first. The desire to win will make it even harder to get the cane to the ground.

Torch tag

This is a great night-time game if you're with a group of people when camping, providing you have an area to play it that you know is perfectly safe. But it will work equally well in a large garden.

It is a variant of tag with 'It' using a torch instead of having to touch people. Players should wear dark clothing, the better to hide themselves. They may even blacken their faces with camo cream or burnt cork, providing Dad's happy to oblige by first opening a bottle of wine with an old-fashioned cork. A base is set up, ideally in the centre of the playing area, from which everyone scatters. While 'It' counts to the agreed number, players should hide, though they must keep within the agreed playing area.

'It' then goes hunting with the torch. If they shine the light on somebody and call out their name then that person is caught and must return to the base. Those who are caught can be rescued. If a player gets to the base they can release the first of the players who's been caught there; they then have 30 free seconds to hide themselves again.

If 'It' fails to call out a name or gets a name wrong, the person they've tried to tag must yell out that they've made a mistake and has 30 seconds free to hide themselves. They can't use that time for rescuing another player.

'It's task is to get all the players into the base, though you might want to set a time limit. If the group is particularly large and you have a plentiful supply of torches and batteries, two or more people can be 'It' to even up the chances.

We'll be safe here,
I've hidden the
batteries

One-and-a-half-a-side football

Playing football is great if you have plenty of kids – but if there are only three of you, it can be tricky to divide the sides up equally. Solomon had one answer to this conundrum, but we don't recommend slicing your offspring in half.

We find the best method is to have one player in goal, leaving two out on the field. One of these is the attacker, one the defender. If the defender manages to tackle the attacker and gain possession of the ball, then he becomes the attacker and the attacker becomes the defender.

Once someone scores, they go in goal, and the former goalie comes out to be the attacker. It's a neat solution to an otherwise tricky problem.

Swimming pool games

These days you're not allowed to do anything in public swimming pools that might possibly constitute fun, for 'health and safety' reasons. (Much as we'd like to, this isn't the place to go into a rant about *that* subject.) But if you're on holiday, perhaps staying in a villa with a pool, then you're going to spend a lot of time in it with your kids: here are a couple of ideas to increase the fun.

Pool basketball is a game we've enjoyed over the years, and has the great advantage that it doesn't require a basket. You'll need a soft ball, slightly larger than a tennis ball: sports shops sell small rugby balls, about 20 cm long, that are ideal for this purpose (although if you can't find one, then a tennis ball will do).

Divide the players into two teams, and give the ball to one of them. The rules are simple: you have to throw the ball between players on the same team, and the other team has to intercept it and then throw it between themselves. It's a family-friendly game in which everyone can join in, since Dad can always make sure the ball gets passed to the smallest players frequently.

Underwater football is another good pool game. You'll need an old, punctured football: fill it with water by holding it underwater and expelling all the air. If you leave it for half an hour or so, it should fill with water by itself, regaining something approaching its original shape. Now play football with it, *in slow motion*: all the fun of an action replay, without any of the irritating commentary.

Acrobatic backflips are easy and fun, as long as your kids are small enough. They face you, with their arms around your neck and their legs bent, resting their feet on your hands. On the count of three, you lift upwards as they straighten their legs and throw themselves back: with a bit of practice, they can achieve quite spectacular somersaults in the air. Do make sure there's no one directly behind them when you do this, of course.

Football balancing involves a football for each player. They have to push it down so they're sitting on it – this can be quite tricky, as the ball will be very buoyant and will try to push itself up past them. Once they've managed this, their next task is to push the ball down so they're standing on it. It takes skill and delicate balancing: one advantage is that the smaller the child, the less deep the ball has to go, and so the easier it becomes.

Next time can I fly first class, Daddy?

Is it a bird? No, it's a plane

Lie on your back and, holding their hands to keep them steady, let your child lie on your upturned feet. Your feet should rest on their abdomen, their centre of gravity. Hold their hands or wrists as they climb on, until they feel comfortable. Once they're balanced, get them to put their legs out straight behind them and let go of your hands, holding their armsoutwards. Hurrah! They're flying! As they become more confident, you can move your legs from side to side and extend them so they fly high up the air – at least it will seem so to them.

This is one for relatively young children. Once they're coming round for Sunday lunch with your grandchildren in tow, you might want to consider giving it up.

Camping food

Kids seem to love camping. The hard, lumpy ground, the hours spent watching Dad struggling with a tent whose assembly instructions have been imperfectly translated from the original Korean, the sensation of having your extremities nibbled by hitherto undiscovered species of venomous insect in the middle of the night, and above all the cold when the anaesthetic campfire beers finally wear off at three o'clock in the morning. Don't you just love it?

There's always the recourse to food, to make the pain a little more bearable. Here are a few of our tried and tested campfire recipes. You *can* cook them over a barbecue; but a real campfire is more fun for everyone.

Chocolate bananas

Keeping the skin on, slit a banana most of the way through along its length. Break chocolate up into pieces and push them into the slit. It doesn't matter if they are sticking out a little.

Wrap the banana completely in foil and place it on your fire, Trangia or Primus and leave it there until the foil is completely black. Open up the foil and spoon out the disgustingly mushy, but yummily delicious choconana mix inside.

Izzy's chocolate digestive marshmallows

The bigger the better when it comes to toasting marshmallows around a campfire. Rather than use any utensils you've brought with you, it's much better to get the children to use twigs. Try to ensure, though, that they're not too long dead. If there's no green left inside, you'll suddenly find that the whole twig is ablaze and gets dropped into the fire. A waste of a good marshmallow.

Izzy's preferred way of toasting marshmallows is to shove it completely into the fire. That way, it gets covered in ash. When it's nicely melted, pull it out, blow or scrape off the ash and put the gooey marshmallow between two chocolate digestive biscuits. Naturally, when you get home, you should tell their mum that they've eaten nothing but salad and protein the entire time.

Camp doughnuts

This is a international favourite with Scouts and Guides around the world, no doubt because they know it's the sort of thing that would give health-conscious parents palpitations. They are unquestionably delicious, though, and if the children *are* getting plenty of fresh air and exercise, why not give them a whirl – they're bound to need a blood sugar boost at some point.

There might be campers keen enough to make the pancake batter mix needed from scratch with flour, milk and eggs, but it's far easier to use the packet stuff. Make up jam sandwiches (using white bread, naturally). Dunk them in the pancake batter then fry them in oil until they're golden. Whip them out, dip them in white sugar and serve them to appreciative, hungry campers. You might even consider adding these to your barbecue recipe list as a treat for the kids.

If you are cooking in a pan on an open fire, it's worth knowing that if you rub washing-up liquid on the underneath of the pan first, it will be a great deal easier to clean later.

Dampers

This perennial camping favourite is a simple form of bread, originating in the Australian outback. Mix up ten parts of self-raising flour with three parts of water, a sprinkle of salt and a little sugar, kneading the dough.

Roll the dough into long fingers. Find some strong sticks and twist the dough around them in a spiral, cooking over an open fire if you have one, but again a barbecue is also fine. Try not to make the snakes too thick or the outside will burn before the inside is cooked.

Fun though this is, bear in mind that the dough is relatively tasteless, so you might want to try some variations. Cook a sausage on a stick, for instance, wrap dough around it and bake it in the fire. Or put some chocolate spread in the snake of dough before you twist it around the stick. Wrapped in foil, loaves or patties can be cooked in the embers of a fire.

Campfire songs

For some reason, the very act of being out in the open at night, huddled up to a roaring fire, seems to bring out the community spirit and the desire to burst into song in even the most reserved of families. Just in case this should happen to you, it helps to know the words to at least a few songs.

The Quartermaster's Stores

This, one of the most popular of all campfire songs, probably originated in the services, but it doesn't *have* to be ribald. The best thing about it is that it's easy even for children to make up new lines in the middle of the song. Give them a bit of warning and they should be able to come up with lines about the other members of the group ('There was Steve, Steve, bogeys on his sleeve', etc).

There are rats rats big as al ley cats In the stores, in the stores There are rats, rats,

big as al ley cats In the Quar ter mas ter's stores My eyes a re dim I   can not see I

have no t brought my specs with me I   have no t brought my   specs with   me

There are rats, rats, big as alley cats
In the stores, in the stores.
There are rats, rats, big as alley cats
In the Quartermaster's stores.

Chorus:
My eyes are dim, I cannot see
I have not brought my specs with me
I have not brought my specs with me

Continue with the following verses, repeating the same 'eyes are dim' chorus each time:

There are mice, mice, running through the rice...

There are snakes, snakes, as big as garden rakes....

There is cheese, cheese, that brings you to your knees...

There is gravy, gravy, enough to float the navy...

There are cakes, cakes, that give us tummy aches...

There is butter, butter, running in the gutter...

There is bread, bread, with great big lumps like lead...

There are bees, bees, with little knobby knees...

There are apes, apes, eating all the grapes...

There are turtles, turtles, wearing rubber girdles...

There are bears, bears, with curlers in their hair...

There are buffaloes, buffaloes, with hair between their toes...

There are foxes, foxes, stuffed in little boxes...

There is Coke, Coke, enough to make you choke...

There are flies, flies, swarming round the pies...

There are fishes, fishes, washing all the dishes...

Head, Shoulders, Knees and Toes

Songs with actions are a great way of keeping warm when the flames begin to die out. Here's an old classic that's still fun to sing.

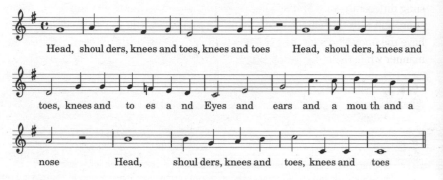

Head, shoulders, knees and toes, knees and toes
Head, shoulders, knees and toes, knees and toes and
Eyes and ears and a mouth and a nose
Head, shoulders, knees and toes, knees and toes

Head, shoulders, knees and toes, knees and toes.
Head, shoulders, knees and toes, knees and toes and
Eyes and ears, and a mouth and a nose.
Head, shoulders, knees and toes, knees and toes.

It looks delightfully ridiculous when everyone touches the body part mentioned. It gets still better if, with each successive singing, one more body part is omitted, though still touched. The penultimate time around, only the word 'and' is heard. The final time, it should be sung in full but incredibly quickly.

Forty Years on an Iceberg

The fun in this song comes from everyone doing the actions together. In a similar way to Heads, Shoulders, Knees and Toes, sometimes the subsequent verses are sung differently, with first one line, then two and so on hummed rather than being sung, still with the actions being made. Or you could split the group into two and have the ones who sing the two lines of 'Buh duh duh da da da' continuing in like manner while the other group sings.

Forty years on an iceberg *(make the number 10 four times with your hands)*
Over the ocean wide *(make waves with your hands)*
Nothing to wear but pyjamas *(pull up the shoulders of whatever you're wearing)*
Nothing to do but slide...WEEEEEE! *(pretend to dive)*
The wind was cold and blustery *(shiver with your arms crossed)*
The frost began to bite! *(pinch a neighbour)*
I had to hug my polar bear *(hug your neighbour)*
To keep me warm at night, Oh!
Buh duh duh da da da
Buh duh duh da da da

If I Were Not Upon the Stage

If you're prepared to put in a little effort, working up a version of this song with your children and perhaps a few of their friends could be one of the most hilarious things you'll ever do. The song is popular on cruise liners as 'If I were not upon the Seas', as well as with Boy Scouts and Girl Guides singing what they'd do if they weren't. The tune is academic and often seems to be more chanted than sung.

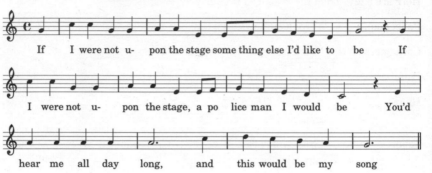

If I were not u- pon the stage some thing else I'd like to be If

I were not u- pon the stage, a po lice man I would be You'd

hear me all day long, and this would be my song

If I were not upon the stage something else I'd like to be.
If I were not upon the stage, a (*profession*) I would be.
You'd hear me all day long, and this would be my song.

At this point, the singer has not only to yell out the cry of their chosen profession for two bars, but also to act it out. The trick is to come up with professions that involve daft gesticulations and cries as well as spreading over into the space of the person next to them.

So a policeman, for instance, might direct traffic with 'move along now, move along now. Passing to the right', putting out their right hand as they do the 'passing to the right'. This would hit their neighbour, were the neighbour not perhaps a carpenter. They might 'nail it up here, nail it down there, nail it to the floor', bending over to hit an imaginary nail into the floor just as the policeman extends their hand.

As more professions are introduced, you might have someone who doesn't get out of the way of the person next to them. A window cleaner with a sponge might wash the face or glasses of the person next to them, who could be a referee removing their glasses the better to stare myopically at the ball. Adult versions of this can tend towards the bawdy. You need to establish if you want any of this. You might all think that someone inadvertently goosing their neighbour as they bend down is fine. It's up to you.

The new profession is introduced alone each time. Then, after they've done their cry once, they continue it as the previous person joins in, followed by the one before them, and so on, until everybody does it together, at which point a new person comes on 'stage'. The kids should enjoy coming up with ideas of their own. Here are a few to get the creative juices flowing.

Policeman: 'Move along now, move along now. Passing to the right.'

Carpenter: 'Nail it up here, nail it down there, nail it to the floor.'

Plumber: 'Plunge it. Flush it. Look out down below.'

Hippy: 'Love and peace. Joy to the world. Cool, man. Far out. Wow.' (making peace signs)

Tailor: 'Chest thirty-two. Waist forty-six. Cutting it to size.' (making snip snip actions to the side)

Shop assistant: 'Four ninety-nine. Here's your change. Have a nice day, sir.' (holding out the change at the end)

Banker: 'Charging for this, charging for that. Banking's really interesting.' (It's fun if the banker reaches out to take the money from the shop assistant. Or have a politician instead of a banker.)

Lifeguard: 'Save yourself, man, I'm a busy guy. I'm working on my tan.'

Painter: 'Open the tin, stir the paint. Slap it on the wall.'

Fireman: 'Jump, lady, jump. We'll catch you. Whoops. Splat.' (looking up and then, rapidly, down, pulling away an imaginary net)

Aerobics teacher: 'Arms up, arms down. Hips left, hips right.' (knocking their hips into the neighbour on one side, then the other)

Teacher: 'Sit down. Shut up. Throw away your gum.'

Airline steward: 'Stay in your seat. Do up your belt. Here's your sick bag. BLEH!'

Electrician: 'Neutral's blue. Brown is live. So what's this one here do? Argghh.' (miming being electrocuted)

Ging Gang Gooley

Legend has it that this perennial but nonsensical Scout and Guide song was conjured up by Robert Baden-Powell himself for the first World Scout Jamboree in 1920 so that Scouts, whatever their native tongue, could sing it. For the jamboree, the exhibition hall at Olympia was filled with earth a foot thick which was then turfed, enabling the Scouts to put up their tents in the glass-roofed hall.

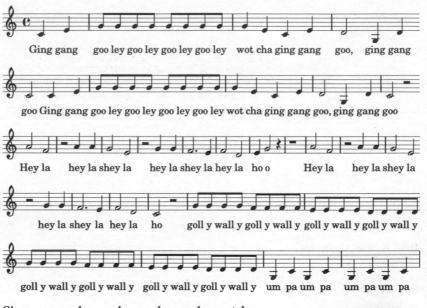

Ging gang goo ley goo ley goo ley goo ley wot cha ging gang goo, ging gang

goo Ging gang goo ley goo ley goo ley goo ley wot cha ging gang goo, ging gang goo

Hey la hey la shey la hey la shey la hey la ho o Hey la hey la shey la

hey la shey la hey la ho goll y wall y goll y wall y goll y wall y goll y wall y

goll y wall y goll y wall y goll y wall y goll y wall y um pa um pa um pa um pa

Ging gang gooley, gooley, gooley, gooley, watcha
Ging gang goo, ging gang goo.
Ging gang gooley, gooley, gooley, gooley, watcha
Ging gang goo, ging gang goo.
Heyla, heyla sheyla, heyla shey-la, heyla ho
Heyla, heyla sheyla, heyla shey-la, heyla ho
Golly wally, golly wally, golly wally, golly wally
Um-pa, Um-pa, Um-pa.

6 Dad in the kitchen

THERE COMES A TIME IN EVERY DAD'S LIFE when he has to venture into the kitchen. (It's that room at the end of the corridor, which often has delicious smells emanating from it. If you still can't find it, ask your kids.)

We're not suggesting that all Dads are incompetent cooks, by any means. But it's a sad fact that many of us are less adept at the culinary arts than we (or our partners) would like.

Next time you have the kids to yourself for a time, rather than cracking open a six-pack of ready meals, try cooking something using raw ingredients. We've a selection of easy but tasty recipes that will fill them up a treat, while restoring your reputation as the Dad who really *can* do everything.

There's more fun to be had in the kitchen than just making food, of course. So we've also thrown in a selection of experiments, activities and assorted nonsense that you can do using everyday foodstuffs.

The recipes

For those occasions when Dad is left to feed the family, here are some easy and tasty ideas to keep the wolf from the door (and the kids from the biscuit tin).

GRILLED FISH SNACKS

Frozen fish fillets	*Tomatoes*
Dry cider	*Cheddar cheese*

Although those Dads who don't fancy themselves as budding Jamie Olivers think of fish as being fiddly to cook, this tasty recipe can be whipped up in next to no time with little preparation. Next time you're in a supermarket (making sure to have your phone with you, of course, so you can call your partner to ask where things are), grab some skinned fish fillets. White fish like cod, haddock or halibut is what you're after. Forget the fresh-fish counter and instead pick up ungarnished, unbattered frozen blocks and shove them in your freezer.

Get out as many as there are mouths to feed. The only other preparation needed is to slice a tomato or two thinly, doing the same with some cheddar cheese. You could grate the cheese, but that means cleaning a cheese grater afterwards. Do you really want to bother? Have a bottle of dry cider ready – you may as well pour yourself a glass while you're at it.

Proper cooks will butter the grill pan to stop the fish sticking. Dads who loathe washing up should shove foil in it instead, making sure it curves upwards on all sides to keep the juices in. Rub a knob of butter over the foil, leaving it in the pan under the grill to melt while you defrost the fish in the microwave.

Salt the defrosted fish then shove it into the grill pan, spooning the melted butter over it. Cook it on one side for three minutes or so, then turn it over and spoon the juices over it. Pour one tablespoon of cider over each fillet and cook for another three minutes. Don't worry, the alcohol will burn off.

Add the slices of tomato and cheese and keep cooking until the cheese has melted, probably another three or four minutes. Then serve.

As long as the foil hasn't torn, you can simply dispose of it, happy that there's no necessity to wash the grill pan.

FRENCH TOAST

Sliced bread	*Eggs*
Milk	*Oil or butter*
Cinnamon sugar	*Maple syrup or tinned fruit*

This recipe is also commonly known as 'eggy bread'. But how much more exotic and delicious it sounds when given a continental flavour. In the United States, they tried to change the name to 'freedom toast'.

For each five pieces of French toast, you need three medium sized eggs. Beat the eggs, adding enough milk to swell the mixture by about 25 per cent. Locate a big shallow dish and pour in the mixture. Get your bread ready. The white, sliced stuff we're told isn't good for us seems to make the best French toast. Indeed bread that's too stale for toast or sandwiches is perfectly fine, just so long as it isn't actually mouldy. We keep the slices intact, others prefer to half or quarter them, enabling you to get more in the frying pan.

Add vegetable oil or butter (our preference) to a frying pan until it's melted and the whole pan is greased. Using a fork, dip a piece of bread into the mixture so that it soaks it up, turning the bread over if the mixture isn't deep enough to do both sides at once.

Put this, and as many similarly treated others as you can fit, into the frying pan. Turn them over after a couple of minutes. You're aiming for a golden brown colour. If they're burnt, you've gone a bit too far and know to pull the next batch out more quickly.

Put the cooked French toast on to sheets of kitchen roll to cut down on their greasiness. Continue frying with more bread until the mixture is all used up. Keep adding enough butter or oil to the pan to prevent burning but not so much that the bread drowns in it.

Eggy bread is particularly nice served with cinnamon sugar (mix powdered cinnamon with sugar if you haven't any), maple syrup or even fruit such as strawberries or tinned peach slices.

FRIED MATZO

7 matzo sheets	4 eggs
Milk	Oil or butter

Matzo, or unleavened bread, was apparently invented when the Jews got fed up with building pyramids for the Egyptians and fled the country with the army in hot pursuit. They were in such a rush that they didn't have time to let their bread rise and so discovered they'd made a crunchy, thin cracker. Matzo is now promoted as a healthy snack, being 98 per cent fat free and with no added salt. But it's a doddle to negate such health benefits with this delicious teatime treat.

Matzo is available in most supermarkets and many convenience stores, usually among the crackers. It's best to use the rectangular matzos in the big box. If you can't find any, try water biscuits instead.

For three to four people with healthy appetites use the seven sealed sheets that make up half the box's contents. Break them up in a colander until they're in bite-size pieces. Do this in a sink as there will be lots of crumbs. Soak the matzo with hot running water for two or three minutes until it's soft but not completely squishy, then shake it around to help the excess water drain off.

Break three eggs into a mixing bowl along with a small amount of milk and beat the mixture. Mix in the well-drained matzo so that it absorbs the eggs.

Add butter (or vegetable oil) to a hot, non-stick frying pan and spoon in the gooey matzo, spreading it around the pan. Stir it fairly often, occasionally adding more butter to stop it sticking and burning. Fry until golden brown and just going crispy at the edges.

We serve it with added salt to taste. Others season it with cinnamon sugar, syrup, fruit or jam and we've also heard of people cooking it with bananas, grating cheese over it towards the end of cooking and even adding mushrooms, peppers and the like and treating it as a stir fry.

Fried matzo is a doddle to make, though cleaning all the matzo mess from the colander afterwards isn't our favourite chore.

EGG IN A CUP

2 eggs	*1 slice of bread*
Butter	*Salt and pepper*

This is a great favourite, especially when our kids are feeling unwell and need a comfort snack in bed. It's dead easy to make, and goes down a treat with kids of all ages.

Boil the eggs so they're still soft inside (three minutes from boiling!). Butter the bread, and cut into small squares. Then mix the whole lot together in a large teacup (remembering to scoop the egg out of the shells first), adding a little salt and pepper to taste.

ANCHOVY SPAGHETTI

1 tin anchovies	*Spaghetti*

There aren't many recipes whose title contains all the ingredients, but cooking doesn't get much simpler than this. It really helps if your kids like anchovies, of course, and we realise that many don't.

First, boil up some spaghetti. It takes about 12 minutes. Tip the anchovies out of the tin and into a small frying pan. No need to add oil as they're already swimming in it. Cook until the anchovies dissolve into a brownish paste, then pour into the spaghetti and mix well. It tastes a lot better than it sounds!

STEVE'S SUPER SLIPPERY SLURPY SOUP SHOP SPECIAL

1 tbsp powdered chicken soup mix	*2 pints water*
Half packet rice noodles	*4 slices of ham*
3 carrots	*1 onion*

Thinly slice the carrots and the onion, and fry them in a large saucepan until the onion goes soft. Add shredded ham, all the water, and the chicken soup mix. When the water boils, add the rice noodles, and stir for about five minutes until the noodles soften. Absolutely delicious.

The surprising world of tomato ketchup

Derived from the chinese *ke-tsiap*, ketchup would originally have tasted very different, being a savoury pickled fish sauce akin to the likes of Worcestershire or soy sauce. It was brought to Europe in the 17th century by sailors but early ingredients might have included mushrooms, oysters, lobsters or anchovies. The word 'ketchup' first appeared in 1711 but other spellings like catsup or catchup were common too.

Early ketchups in colonial America were savoury but the Americans' sweet teeth were indulged in the mid-19th century with various sweetened tomato ketchups. In 1876, H. J. Heinz added one to his product line and never looked back.

The Americans have regulations governing the flow of ketchup, which must ooze between 3 and 7 centimetres in 30 seconds. If it doesn't, it can't call itself 'ketchup'.

Ketchup has recently been discovered to be healthy as it – along with other processed tomato products – contains lycopene, which apparently helps in fighting some cancers. Organic ketchup, of course, is the healthiest of all.

In 2000, Heinz started making coloured ketchups in the hope of appealing to children. But kids didn't take to green, purple, pink, orange, blue or teal ketchup (only green was available in the UK), so they were abandoned.

The world's largest ketchup bottle is a water tower built in the shape of a sauce bottle at a former ketchup bottling plant in 1949 in Illinois. It stands 170 feet tall. Incidentally, ketchup is also great for cleaning copper! Smear it on and leave it to do its magic for ten minutes before rinsing off.

Getting ketchup out of the bottle

Everyone knows how difficult it is to get ketchup out of a glass bottle. The new squeezy bottles, particularly those designed to be stored upside-down, take all the fun out of the process. Luckily many restaurants still serve it in bottles, giving Dad a chance to show off. Ketchup, of course, is very viscous and tends to stick to the inside of the bottle, a property scientists call thixotropic.

The standard way of trying to get ketchup out involves hitting the inverted bottom of the bottle but the restaurant trade has long known a better way. It

involves tapping the neck of the bottle, held only slightly downwards (as you would when you pour any other liquid), onto a fist or open hand. If it's Heinz, the 57 circle on the neck is exactly the right spot.

This method not only helps air get into the bottle to free the ketchup but also gives it some downward impetus when the bottle stops on striking the hand. The correct way of getting ketchup out of the bottle, it seems, is all down to G-forces.

Why is an ice cream with a Flake in called a 99?

Cadbury's introduced the Flake in 1920 (presumably using only the crumbliest, flakiest chocolate). In 1928, one of their sales managers saw some Italian ice-cream makers cutting them in half to sell with ice cream. So Cadbury's produced a shorter Flake in 1930, specifically intended to be shoved into an ice-cream cone at a jaunty 45-degree angle. By the mid-1930s, this combination was known as a 99.

Nobody, though, seems to know exactly why it's called 99. In roman numerals, IC (Ice Cream) can be 99, though it's more usual as XCIX. The boxes of Flakes for the ice-cream trade cost six shillings and sixpence, written as 6/6 which, upside down, would look like 99. Others have suggested that there were 99 mini-Flakes in each box or that the cornets of the time were stamped with '99'.

There may be no definitive answer, so just enjoy them. For chocoholics, even better than one Flake is two, known for rather obvious reasons as 'Bunny Ears'. When Simon was growing up, you normally asked for a '99 with monkey blood' which meant you wanted loads of raspberry syrup on it too.

Music in the kitchen

Right, that's the recipes and food facts out of the way – now let's get on to the fun stuff. To the resourceful Dad, a kitchen is a toolbox of ideas: more fun can be had in here (with your kids) than just about any other room in the house. Our first few examples are all about making music with everyday kitchen items.

Bottle blowing

Bottles are wonderful music-makers. If you have enough filled with different levels of liquid, you can play them by blowing across their open tops: hold them against your lips and blow straight across. The bigger the bottle, the deeper the pitch.

Still too high – better drink some more

If you want to fine-tune the pitch, add a little water to the empty bottle to make it sound a little higher. Give a differently pitched bottle to each child, and you've got yourself an orchestra.

A wine bottle makes a splendidly bass-like accompaniment, though the less full the bottle, and the more you've drunk of it, the better the music seems to sound.

The straw oboe

We showed in *Dad Stuff* how to make the noise of a duck with a straw. But you can use straws in other ways, particularly the fat kind you tend to get in fast food joints. Instead of making a V-cut, flatten the straw at one end. You can do this in your mouth by biting it around an inch of the way in, and then pulling it out of your

mouth while flattening it with your teeth. Cut half an inch or so along the fold on each side of the straw.

Put it in your mouth, pressing the two halves together with your lips, and blow. This is effectively a double reed, as used for playing oboes and bassoons and these are notoriously tricky to get a good note from, as the parents of any budding oboeist will tell you. So a bit of experimentation is needed. If you can't get it to work, stick the straw further into your mouth and blow, and you get something curiously similar to the duck-call maker explained in Dad Stuff.

Penny whistle on the cheap

A whole penny? What a waste! Here's a whistle you can make for almost nothing, again using a simple drinking straw.

Wrap one end of the straw around your finger once or twice, pinching it with the thumb so that you have a firm grip on it. With the straw pointing upwards, blow across it as you would a bottle. Squeeze the straw with the thumb and index finger of your free hand and, by sliding it up and down, you can make a sound like a Swanee whistle, though it's much easier to go up in pitch than to go down again.

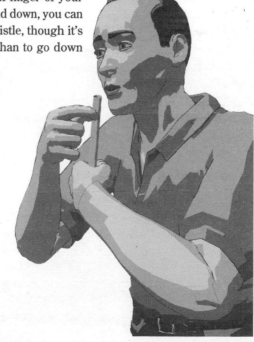

HOW DOES IT WORK?

Both the bottle and the penny whistle work in much the same way as a flute. By blowing, the mouth causes the column of air in them to vibrate. These vibrations are perceived by our ears as a note. The longer the column of vibrating air, the lower the note.

If you experiment with the level of liquid in eight bottles, you can produce a scale over a full octave. Perceptive children will notice that the more liquid and the less air a bottle contains, the higher the note.

Following in Mozart's footsteps

If you have a set of wine glasses, you can make them sing with your finger. Holding the base of the glass with one hand, moisten the index or middle finger of your other hand and rub it around the rim of the glass at a constant speed. Vary the pressure and speed until a note sounds. The better the quality of the glass, the easier it usually is to produce a note and the purer the sound. Crystal, they say, is particularly good but you may think twice about letting your kids loose on your best wedding presents.

The diameter of the bowl matters, too. Flute-style glasses, despite the promising

name, are well-nigh useless. The easiest glasses to get a sound from are those old-fashioned and unstylish ones with the hemispherical bowls. If the glass has traces of slippery washing-up liquid, it will be much harder to play.

Adding water to the wine glass will raise the pitch, and you can tune your glasses to play a recognisable scale.

With some glasses you can actually see the surface of the liquid rotating in the same direction as your finger. Dropping something small that floats will demonstrate this. With certain glasses, moving your finger at a slower rate while pressing harder can create spectacular wave patterns on the surface of the water.

People have been making music with glass for centuries. It became something of a craze in the 18th century. The noted American inventor Benjamin Franklin devised a mechanical glass harmonica with a revolving spindle that did much of the work in 1762 (pictured bottom left) while, in 1791, Mozart composed an adagio for glass harmonica.

People noticed that musicians who specialised in making music with tuned glass often went mad. It wasn't the ethereal music that sent them potty, but the lead with which the rims of the glass were painted. Over time they absorbed the poison through their fingers, just as the Romans had done internally and rather dramatically from their lead plumbing.

HOW DOES IT WORK?

Every object has a natural frequency. The friction created by your finger slipping and sticking hundreds of times a second causes the molecules of the glass to vibrate at its natural, or resonant, frequency.

Although your finger can't impart any more energy than this, a singer hitting the glass's resonant frequency can, which is how some singers can shatter glasses with their voice. Noises that coincide with natural frequencies explain why heavy vehicles driving past a house can make the windows rattle.

Resonance can be a problem for suspension bridges. In 1940, shortly after it was opened, winds caused the Tacoma Narrows bridge in America to begin to vibrate. The vibrations grew bigger until the roadway began buckling, oscillating up and down and from side to side. The bridge literally tore itself to pieces, huge sections falling into the river below. There are amazing videos of this easily locatable on the web.

For this reason, some bridges carry signs warning troops that they must 'break step' when they are crossing. It is the reason that the Millennium Footbridge across the Thames in London had to be closed in 2000 for a time. People walking across were feeling queasy at the way the bridge swayed and the vibrations had to be damped down.

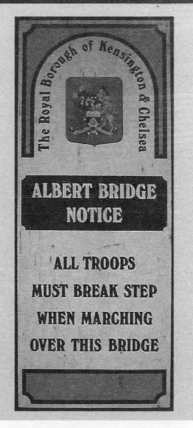

The Royal Borough of Kensington & Chelsea

ALBERT BRIDGE NOTICE

ALL TROOPS MUST BREAK STEP WHEN MARCHING OVER THIS BRIDGE

How to play the spoons

It is one of the sadder facts about Simon that, having been taught to play the spoons as a teenager, he now carries a pair of spoons around with him in case he gets a chance to show off this so-called talent. It seems only fitting that he should pass on this skill so that others may also experience the 'pleasure' of listening to two bits of cutlery being banged together.

Although teaspoons and serving spoons can be used, it's best to learn on dessert spoons (the kind you use for cereal). Assuming you intend playing them right-handed, with the fingers of your hand curled towards your palm, push the

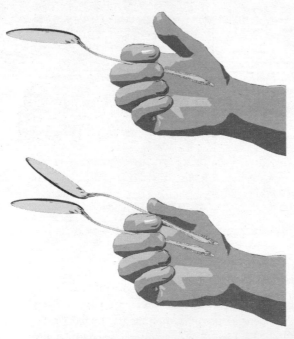

handle of one of the spoons, bowl downwards, between your index and middle fingers. It should be positioned above the first joint of the middle finger with the finger curling back to hold the spoon against your palm.

The other spoon, bowl upwards, should sit on your index finger with the finger curling back to hold the spoon in place. Your thumb should rest along the handle of the spoon, helping to keep it in position. (Those with smaller hands may need to rest the lower spoon on the ring finger rather than the middle.)

With your index finger as a fulcrum, squeeze the ends of the spoons with your palm so that there is a gap of half an inch or so between the bowls of the spoons. Seated, strike the spoons against your leg and they should sound a note. If you're holding the spoons correctly, they should spring apart again. Once you're able to do this, hold your free hand – palm down – above the spoons. Bring them up to strike it, then back down on your leg and so on. You should soon be able to make very fast beats between your hand and your leg, changing where you accent the notes and occasionally beating twice on your palm to each downstroke. Loosening your grip a little, riffle the spoons down the spread fingers of your hand.

Don't use your best spoons for this. Over time, the bowls of the lovely spoons you were given as a wedding present will gradually get flattened. In any case, lightweight, tinny spoons actually give better 'notes' than heavier spoons. Simon prefers to use two different types of spoon, a heavier one on the bottom and a lighter one on top. He was also once told by Martin Ash, aka Sam Spoons of the Bonzo Dog Doo-Dah Band, that wrapping old-style plasters around the handles stops them slipping if your hands get sweaty.

Teach your kids how to play the spoons and they have another invaluable life skill. Who knows how much university will cost by the time they're old enough to go? Now they won't have to serve burgers to help pay for it. They can busk instead, an activity that can be done outdoors, thus ensuring they get plenty of fresh air.

Oi! Keep the noise down out there!

The noisy kitchen

To the average toddler, a kitchen is a percussionist's paradise. Forget buying expensive plastic drum sets that make plastic noises: give them a couple of wooden spoons and a set of saucepans instead. You can even tie a string around a saucepan lid and suspend it from a table to make a passable cymbal. This is the point where kitchen roll comes in handy: wad it up into small pieces, and stuff it in your ears to muffle the noise.

Bog roll kazoo

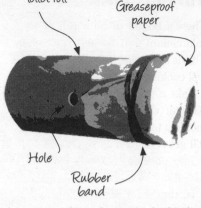

Toilet roll

Greaseproof paper

Hole

Rubber band

Even if your children don't learn any conventional instruments, that's no reason why you can't have musical fun together with the likes of Swanee whistles and kazoos. Swanee whistles are perhaps a little tricky to make yourself but while kazoos are pretty inexpensive to buy, they're also incredibly easy to make, even if they aren't the prettiest-looking of objects.

Get hold of some some waxed or greaseproof paper. There's probably some lying around in a drawer in the kitchen somewhere. That most uncomfortable household item, Izal toilet paper, will also do if you still encounter it anywhere (see, progress *is* a wonderful thing).

Wrap it around the end of an empty loo roll, or half of the inner tube from a kitchen paper or tin foil roll. Fasten the paper in place with a rubber band, ensuring that the paper is tight enough to vibrate. Using something like a pencil, make a hole in the side of the tube for the air to escape and that's it, your kazoo is ready.

The best way of getting a note is not to hum, as people oddly seem to recommend for kazoos, but to sing 'Ahh' into it.

Cornflour magic

Cornflour is weird stuff: when mixed with water, it has the bizarre property of being both gloopy and solid at the same time.

Mix together two cups of cornflour and one cup of water. Place a teaspoon in the glass, and ask your kids to stir the mixture slowly. They'll have no problem, as the consistency will be similar to custard. Then, tell them to stir it quickly, and they'll find they won't be able to: when they try rapid movements, the cornflour mixture will suddenly go solid, preventing the spoon from moving.

Pour some into your hands and, moving fast, roll it into a ball between your palms. As long as you keep rolling, it will form what appears to be a solid ball. Pass it to your children, though, and it will revert to its slushy form, slipping straight through their fingers.

Tin foil masks

There's bound to be a roll of tin foil (aluminium foil) around somewhere. This is a far more interesting use than just cooking with it.

Take a sheet about 30cm square. Sit your child down, and carefully mould it to the shape of their head. It'll get crumpled as you scrunch it into position, but this isn't a bad thing: the more crumpled it is, the better it will mould to the shape of their face, and the stronger it will be.

You don't want to push too hard around the eyes, obviously, and it can be a good idea to make sure they're still breathing occasionally. Use your fingers to press it around the nose and cheekbones: it can help if they open their mouth slightly and grab the foil with their lips, which will help to hold it in place. Pretty soon it should form a shape that approximates their head. You should be able to lift it off without it distorting too much, and you'll end up with a mask that – in profile, at least – looks exactly like your child.

Make your own play dough

Long before Play Doh was available in little plastic pots, parents were mixing the stuff up for themselves. It's easy to make, and you don't have to worry if your kids accidentally swallow some.

Into a kitchen bowl, pour two cups of plain flour, a cup of water, a cup of salt and two tablespoons of cooking oil. You can add a few drops of food colouring if you have any. Mix all the ingredients together with a fork – or with your fingers – and you'll have enough play dough to keep small kids happy for an afternoon. Cut it with cookie cutters, or simply roll it around and mould it into shapes.

The submarine diver

This is a surprisingly good experiment, which shows how small changes in pressure can produce a strong effect. This was sent in to us by *Dad Stuff* reader (and obviously Great Dad) Mark Grant.

bubble of cling film

tied off with cotton

Blutak

To do this trick you'll need an empty mineral water or fizzy drink bottle, some cling film, a piece of cotton and a blob of Blu tak. Try to avoid forcing your kids to drink all the Coke in one go, or you'll have a hard time explaining the burp overdose in Casualty.

Start by cutting a piece of cling film about six inches square, and sucking the middle of it into your mouth (best not to let your kids do this!) to form a bubble of the stuff somewhere between the size of a pea and a walnut. Tie it off with a piece of cotton to make an airtight bulge.

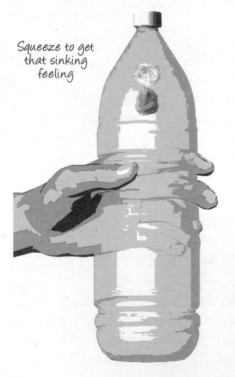

Squeeze to get that sinking feeling

The other end of the cling film will splay out into a sort of fan: this is where you stick the Blu tak. Have a glass of water handy, and place the assembly into the water. It should just about float, so that a tap on the top will send it under only to bob back up: keep adjusting the amount of Blu tak until this works. It's worth taking the time to get the buoyancy right now, as it's hard to extract it from the bottle later.

When the assembly is complete, fill the bottle with water, drop the diver assembly in and screw the lid on tightly. The diver will, of course, float to the top. But here's the clever part: squeeze the bottle, and the diver will sink to the bottom. By varying the pressure with your hand, you can make the diver rise and fall at will: you can even make it float at any position within the bottle. Amazing!

7 The behaviour thing

AS WELL AS ALL THE FUN TIMES to be had, kids do have to learn to do what their parents ask of them. The days of 'wait until your father gets home' are, thankfully, largely behind us, but it's often the case that one parent, more than the other, is responsible for enforcing the dreaded D-word: discipline. And, more often than not, that parent is Dad.

It's an evolution thing. The male of the species has an Adam's apple so he can roar louder, and bigger muscles so he can fend off challenges from young stags. It isn't always Dad who enforces discipline, of course; but, whichever parent the task falls to, we'll give you some useful tips on how to do it with less pain.

The key lies in respecting your children, in recognising that they're not your possessions but people who live with you. Their problems and anxieties are real ones, no matter how trivial owning the newest PlayStation game may seem in comparison with your need to pay the mortgage. Treat them with respect, and they're more likely to respect you in turn.

Keep it simple, part one

Kids love to play games, and one of the best games of all is seeing how far Dad can be pushed before he snaps. If your children dangle your wedding ring over an open drain, or hold a bottle of milk as if they're going to upend it on the carpet, the chances are they're only fooling with you.

Try to resist flying into a sudden rage. It may be what your instinct tells you to do, but it's not necessarily the best solution. Yelling is likely to shock a child into dropping the ring, or spilling the milk, which may well prove your point – but at a cost.

You may regard their actions as irritating, provocative, or just downright idiotic. But unless what they're doing is immediately life-threatening, start with the smallest reaction that will achieve your goal.

Step 1: The eyebrow trick. A comically raised eyebrow is often enough to stop kids in their tracks. It shows them that you've seen what they're up to, and it signifies that their behaviour is inappropriate. The fact that no words have been spoken makes it easier for the child to understand the gesture, and a clear sign is often far more powerful than a barrage of instructions.

Step 2: The head shake. If the eyebrow trick doesn't work, then try simply speaking your child's name. Once you've got their attention, your best course of action is to stay non-verbal as long as you can. A slow shake of the head is a clear, unambiguous statement that every child will understand.

Step 3: Keep their attention. If the actions don't stop after these two interventions, try saying just their name again, with increasing firmness in your voice. And then shake your head again. They know they're doing something they shouldn't, and really don't need you to spell it out for them. Launching into a rant will only confuse them.

Step 4: Explain yourself. Once they've stopped doing whatever it was that started the whole thing off, don't continue to chide them. Instead, explain in as few words as possible why their actions were dangerous or antisocial – and then just leave it at that.

Step 5: Teach them the method. Even if the eyebrow and head shake don't work the first time you try it, it's worth using these two steps each time a minor misdemeanour is in progress. The more you use these techniques, the quicker your child will learn them – and the easier it will be next time.

Keep it simple, part two

If you talk to an adult and they don't understand what you're saying, the usual procedure is to say the same thing in a different way. And to keep on trying different formulations of speech until they get the point.

It doesn't work that way with kids. Mainly because the problem here isn't one of comprehension at all. They know exactly what you want them to do, but they just aren't doing it. This may simply be because it takes longer for them to process the instruction, or because they're doing something else. By constantly changing what you're asking of them, you only add to the confusion.

Here's a typical Dad–Child interchange:

Dad: Put your coat on, we're going out.
Child: (ignores the instruction)
Dad: Put your coat on, it's cold outside.

Child: (no response)

Dad: Come on, your Mum and I both have our coats on.

Child: (no response)

Dad: If you don't put your coat on, you'll catch a cold.

Child: (no response)

Dad: Put your coat on or you won't get to go to the park.

Child: (no response)

Dad: Granny bought you this coat for Christmas, she'd love to know you're wearing it.

Child: She didn't get it for me for Christmas, she got it for my birthday.

Dad: I'm going to get cross if you don't put your coat on right this minute.

See what's happening? Each time you ask your child to put the coat on, you're giving a different reason. You're constantly searching for new ways of saying the same thing, and in doing so you're leading yourself into a trap: your child is all too likely to pick up on a single flaw to defeat your whole argument, which will tend to make you more cross. The less ammunition you give them to use against you, the more success you'll have. Stay consistent: there's only one reason you want them to put their coat on, and that's because it's cold outside.

Of course, knowing this doesn't help you to get them to actually put their coat on; you still need to repeat the instruction. But here's the trick: use fewer words, rather than more. Begin with the instruction, then explain it if necessary; but after that, reduce the number of words you use rather than increasing it.

Here's a better way of holding this rather one-sided exchange:

Dad: Put your coat on.

Child: (no response)

Dad: Put your coat on, it's cold outside.

Child: (no response)

Dad: Put your coat on.

Child: (no response)

Dad: Coat.

Child: (no response)

Dad: Coat.

Eventually, your child will be so ground down that they'll comply with the instruction. They know exactly what you want them to do. All you have to do is to stay as calm as you can!

Don't tell them: show them

Parents often get worked up about table manners, especially when the family's in public or visiting a grandparent. In *Keep it simple*, above, we looked at using gestures to get your point across: the same principle can be applied here.

Nothing's worse for a child than to be humiliated in front of others. So rather than telling them to keep their mouth closed when they chew, instead mime using a finger and thumb to close your own lips. If they're talking with their mouths open, mime dragging a finger down your throat to indicate to them that they should swallow. If they're interrupting an adult conversation, mime putting your finger to your lips and then to your ear, to show that they should listen rather than talk.

It's like a private code between you and your child. It's discreet, easy to understand, and looks like you're reminding them, rather than nagging them. And grandparents will certainly be impressed at how well behaved they are – without having to be reminded!

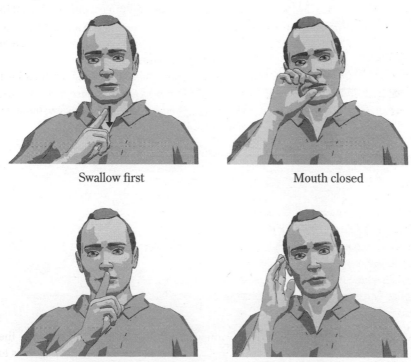

Swallow first

Mouth closed

Don't talk...

...listen!

Yes, no and maybe

Kids ask for things all the time: an ice cream, a trip to Disneyland, a new bike, one more go on the dodgems. They may not appreciate the difference between one that costs a few pence and one that may cost hundreds of pounds.

Before you shoot off a reply, take a beat to consider your answer. 'Yes' always goes down well, but make sure you listen to the question carefully before using this one. 'Maybe' is that old favourite of parents, and it's one of the most useful standbys there is: it gives you time to defer the real answer until you've had time to give it some more thought.

The trouble with saying 'no' straight away is that once you've said it, you really, really do have to stick to it. Otherwise you're likely to end up with this sort of situation:

Child: Can we got to McDonald's?
Dad: No.
Child: I really want to go to McDonald's!
Dad: No, we're going to the pizza place.
Child: I hate pizza. I want a McDonald's.
Dad: No, I've made up my mind.
Child: Please! I really really really want to go to McDonald's!
Dad: No.
Child: If we go to McDonald's, I promise I'll tidy my room when we get home.
Dad: No, we're going for pizza.
Child: Please, Dad, please.
Dad: No, sorry.
Child: Please, please, please, Dad. I love you, Daddy.
Dad: Oh... all right then.

And there, right there, is the single most dangerous phrase a parent can ever use. It slips out so easily, and looks so innocuous, but does all the damage in the world: 'Oh, all right then.'

Once you've used it, your child has won. Worse still, they'll have learned how to win. It may have taken ten minutes to get there, but they beat you down eventually.

So what will happen next time? Exactly the same thing. Except that this time it may take fifteen minutes, or half an hour, or a couple of days. It makes no difference to kids, who have an endless capacity to nag. Once they know that you'll give in eventually, they'll never let up. It may take a little longer each time, but it's worth it: there's an ice cream or a trip to the toyshop at the end of that particular rainbow, and they'll use all the cunning they can muster to get there.

If your child is old enough to understand, then try 'let me think about it' as a first response. Don't be rushed into saying 'no' and then feeling you have to defend your position, unless you're absolutely sure. So be careful before you say 'no'. Because you really do have to mean it.

When you mean No, say so

Many childcare books will tell you that saying 'no' to a child is a negative response, and that you should find other ways to express your intention. Well, try that if you like, but we reckon you're just letting yourself in for an awful lot of bother.

Earlier in this chapter, we looked at why repetition of the same reason is always better than coming up with a different reason each time. The same technique should be used when you want to stop your child playing with a football or skipping in the house, for instance. Again, parents will typically come up with a variety of reasons why indoor football is inappropriate: 'You might break something.' 'You'll burst the ball.' 'You'll get the carpet all muddy.' 'Thierry Henry doesn't play football indoors, and you shouldn't either.'

If your child wants something they really can't have, or shouldn't do, then we recommend saying 'No' first, with a single reason; then repeat that reason; then just stick with No:

Dad: No, you can't play football indoors, you'll break something.
Child: (continues to play)
Dad: No, you'll break something.
Child: (continues to play)
Dad: No.
Child: (continues to play)
Dad: No.

Repetition alone should be enough for your child to stop. Eventually.

Tantrum time

All kids have tantrums. Small kids do it by throwing themselves on the floor and thrashing about, big kids do it by going to their bedrooms and slamming the door. It's the same behaviour, but expressed in different ways.

How you deal with it depends largely on your personal tolerance for humiliation in public places. Certainly, nothing makes the task of dealing with a screaming toddler in a supermarket more difficult than the disapproval of total strangers. Try to ignore their grimaces as much as possible: concentrate on helping your child to deal with the situation.

There are a number of methods for dealing with tantrums. Yelling at them, telling them to snap out of it and shaking your fist in their face is usually counter-productive: and if you've ever seen a grown man yelling at a two-year-old in a pushchair you'll know how absurd it looks.

Here are some of our tried and trusted methods:

Turn them upside down. It's a great mood breaker for under fives, and can usually get them giggling through their tears. Tell them you're going to tip them upside down so that all the anger can fall out, then gently lift them by their waist and turn them over. Ask them, 'Has the anger fallen out yet?' Usually, you'll get a giggly 'Yes'.

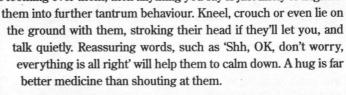

Get down to their level and talk quietly. If your child is rolling around on the floor and you're looming over them, then anything you say is just likely to frighten them into further tantrum behaviour. Kneel, crouch or even lie on the ground with them, stroking their head if they'll let you, and talk quietly. Reassuring words, such as 'Shh, OK, don't worry, everything is all right' will help them to calm down. A hug is far better medicine than shouting at them.

Change the subject. For younger kids especially, distraction is often the best solution. They'll usually be glad of an excuse to get out of their tantrum; becoming interested in an external event allows them to save face, and put the tantrum behind them. Point out an interesting bird in the garden, for example: 'Oh, look, there's a magpie. Over there, on the bush. You can tell it's a magpie, because it's all black and white. Magpies often take shiny things to decorate their nests, you know, so we'd better make sure Mummy's jewellery is locked away…' and so on. Keep on in this vein, and the chances are their interest will be captured. If you can get them to help out – going upstairs to make sure the bedroom window is closed so the magpie can't get the jewellery, for instance – then you'll have achieved your goal.

Be firm, but in control. If the tantrum continues, this could be your signal to move up a gear. 'OK, that'll do now', spoken in a firm tone of voice, is a clear indication that it's time for the display to come to an end. Depending on the age of the child, you can say phrases like 'Stop this, that's enough, we can talk about this' – but be sure to keep an even temper. Don't make it sound as if you're cross, or it will only make things worse. Make it clear you're in control, both of your own emotions and of the situation. Give them a rock to cling to, as it were: the implication is that however bad the situation may be, Dad can deal with it.

Count to three. We don't know why this works, but it frequently does. If a child's in the middle of a tantrum, or about to start on one, say 'one' in a firm, no-nonsense voice, and pause for a couple of seconds. Follow it with 'two', and pause again. On 'three', get up and walk over towards your child. They won't know what's going to happen next, and generally nothing will – except that they'll snap out of the behaviour. It won't work for all children, but it's certainly worth a try.

Ask them what's wrong. It sounds obvious, but it's not a technique most parents even consider. If your child is rolling around on the ground and bashing their fists on the floor, the chances are that something's bothering them. Rather than just telling them to snap out of it, see if they're able to explain what the problem is. A lot of tantrums are caused by children's inability to express their feelings: if you can help them to put their emotions into words, you'll give them a valuable tool with which to deal with them. If they're too young to express themselves coherently, ask them to draw a picture showing how they feel. You may lose a couple of crayons, but it's a small price to pay.

Leave them to it. Removing the audience is a method that's recommended in most textbooks on childcare: 'They're only attention-seeking', runs the advice, 'so withdraw the attention.' It's a solution that works to some extent within the security of your own home, but not one that we've had a lot of success with. When your child is emotionally overwrought, they need your help. Turning your back may work for some parents, but it's not an option we'd recommend.

Be ridiculous

Kids love seeing adults making fools of themselves. It's a technique that can often be used effectively to get them out of a tantrum: placing a saucepan on your head, or taking your socks and shoes off and putting them on your hands, will get most young children laughing – and they'll find it hard to laugh and scream at the same time. Once they start to giggle, you're on a winning streak.

Let's say your child has crawled under the table and is refusing to come out. You could just stand there insisting, but it probably won't do any good. Instead, sit under the table with them, and try conversation along these lines:

Dad: What do you think these table legs are made of?
Child: (no response)
Dad: Are they made of glass?
Child: (no response – but an absurd suggestion is going to grab their attention)
Dad: Maybe they're made of water. Do you think they're water?
Child: No.
Dad: So what are they made of? Paper?
Child: No.
Dad: What do you think they're made of?
Child: Wood.
Dad: Hmm. Wood, eh? Could be. Let's have a look at the top, and see if that's made of wood as well.

(Dad comes out from under the table, and examines the top)

Dad: No, I think the top's made of fur.
Child: No, it's wood, silly.
Dad: Really? It looks like fur to me.

At this point, your child should come out from under the table to look at the surface. The absurd suggestions have provided enough distraction to bring the tantrum to an end, and you can get on with your lives.

Making ridiculous comments is also a good way to stop kids from damaging household objects – something they're only doing to show how much, at that moment, they want to hurt you. Let's say your child has got hold of a pair of scissors, and is preparing to cut a hole in the carpet.

Here's an exchange that can defuse the situation:

Dad: Oh, dear. That's not going to be good. I'd better call a carpet repair man.
Child: (no response)
Dad: Looks like it's going to be too serious for that. I think I should call an ambulance instead.
Child: (pauses for a moment, wondering what's going on)
Dad: Or a lion tamer. Yes, on second thoughts I think a lion tamer is the best solution.

The more absurd you are, the more chance you have of turning the situation around. Use your imagination!

Give them a choice

Young children have very little control over their own lives. They don't decide when to go to bed, where to go on holiday, which school to go to, or even which clothes are bought for them. As they get older, they take on more responsibility and are allowed to make more decisions: but it's still nowhere near enough. It's no wonder kids rebel against direct instructions so often: saying 'no' is about the only option they have.

One way of making them feel better about themselves – and of getting them to do what you want – is to give them a choice of two different courses of action. So rather than saying, for instance, 'There are your clothes – now get dressed', let them become part of the decision process. Don't insist they wear the shirt you've laid out, but give them a choice between two different ones. It's a small inconvenience for you, but it can be very empowering for the child.

Once they've got used to the idea of making choices, you can turn the situation to your advantage. So instead of 'Go and tidy your room', offer them a couple of options. Tell them they can either tidy their room, or do the washing up. Neither is all that palatable, but at least they'll have made the decision themselves.

Keep the choices direct, and simple. And give them the opportunity to make choices whenever possible: it will help them to feel they've been consulted, and that not all of life's decisions have been taken out of their hands.

Kiss and make up

However good a parent you are, however calm and in control, there are times when you'll simply fly off the handle and start yelling. Fair enough: Dads are people too. We can also be hurt and upset.

If you yell, you can certainly expect them to yell back. It's not necessarily a bad thing, and can help to clear the air: getting out all your frustrations and pent-up anger every now and again can make for a more healthy relationship.

The important thing is not to let it linger. Sulking is a bad habit to get into. If one or other of you has stormed out of the room, leave it ten minutes and then go and apologise. It really doesn't matter if you don't think the argument was your fault: apologise anyway. Not for whatever the cause of the problem was, but for yelling.

We'd strongly recommend a hug at this stage. If it seems appropriate, when things have calmed down you can then go on to explain just what it was that made you so cross in the first place: but be sure to listen to the other side of the argument as well.

Invent code words

If you've followed the advice in 'Kiss and make up' and found it works for you, then there's a valuable extra step you can take to avoid exactly the same argument cropping up again, and that's to recall the situation with a code word.

Let's say you've been arguing over whether or not your child should try the Thai curry you've so lovingly prepared. (It sounds trivial, but it's exactly this sort of mundane occurrence that leads to the biggest bust-ups.) You've both yelled, stormed out and slammed the door, and now calmed down. A couple of hugs later, you've discussed the situation and come to a reasonable conclusion: that you, as a Dad, promise not to force your child to eat food they really find disgusting; in return, they'll try at least a mouthful of new foods with an open mind, just in case they find they like it.

So you invent the code words 'Thai curry'. The next time you feel a similar disagreement coming on – which may be about going to see a movie with no car chases in it, or visiting a museum, or reading a book that you enjoyed when you were their age – just say 'Thai curry'. With any luck, both of you will be able to recall the earlier situation, and act accordingly.

Of course, the code words work both ways. So if your child really hates *Swallows and Amazons* you must be prepared to accept the Thai curry argument as well.

Give positive attention

Kids do many things that annoy us. They also do a lot of stuff that's calculated specifically to annoy us – or so it seems. In reality, they're just trying to get our attention. Celebrities will tell you that all publicity is good publicity, and so it is with kids: any attention is often better than none at all.

So if your child is irritating you by, say, constantly tapping their fingers, telling them to stop tapping is feeding their need. A better method is to reward them for *not* tapping, by giving them the attention instead. Rather than saying 'Stop tapping', try saying 'Be still' instead – placing your hand gently on theirs to hold it. When they stop, reward them with 'Good', and a smile of encouragement.

Then, of course, you have to address why they were so desperate to get your attention in the first place. Chances are, they were being missed out of the conversation: so instead of immediately resuming your discussion about the relative merits of a variety of broadband suppliers, take a moment to discuss something of relevance to them.

Reward good behaviour

One way of recognising – and so rewarding – good behaviour is to set up a Star Chart system. Exactly how it works is up to you, but here's a method that we found successful.

We made a set of stars about two inches across, cut out of blue cardboard. Half of them were sprayed gold. A hole was punched in each one, and a peg board made

that would hold the stars. Then we hung it on the kitchen wall, and explained the rules to our kids.

They would get a blue star every time they did something exceptional – such as doing the washing up, or remembering to clean their teeth, or behaving well when Grandma came for tea. When they had five blue stars, they'd get a gold star, and a small prize: this was often a Kinder Egg in our case. When they had five gold stars, they'd then get a big prize – perhaps a sum of money to spend on a toy of their choice. The prizes and amounts depend, of course, on the age of the children.

We found this system enormously effective, and it lasted from the age of about three until verging on teens.

Let reasoned argument succeed

It may sound obvious, but if your kids have a reasonable point, it's worth listening. Say you tell them it's time for bed while they're watching *The Simpsons*. They'll point out that it's halfway through, and it will only be another fifteen minutes – can't they watch till the end? They promise to go to bed the moment it ends.

It's a fair request, which won't seriously upset their night time routine. Rather than insisting they stop what they're doing and comply with your instructions immediately, let yourself be won over by their reasoning, and let them *see* that this is what's happened. Apart from making for an evening devoid of yelling, it will show them that you're a reasonable person, and that you respect their views. All of which will make life easier in the future!

One at a time

When a child of any age is behaving badly, or needs to be told off for any reason, it's often the cue for all the adults in the vicinity to jump in and start telling them off as well.

It's a disastrous approach, of course. Not only will the child feel – perhaps rightly – that everyone's against them, they'll also simply block out all the noise and ignore the instructions.

One adult should be in charge at any one time, and only one. It's clearer for the children, and it's easier for all the other adults concerned. Plus, of course, there's the significant bonus that those who are not on duty can relax without having to worry about enforcing discipline.

Lighten up!

If this chapter makes the whole childcare thing sound like a nightmare, it needn't be so. Kids have a sense of humour, and they'll enjoy joking with you and playing jokes on you. Enjoy their company, recognise when they're being silly for the sake of it, and join in the fun.

8 Teach your child how to think

ALL CHILDREN LIKE PUZZLES. They're great for stimulating the brain: they get the little grey cells working overtime, stimulating the parts that TV and video games cannot reach.

But kids often need help working through a complex puzzle. You can't just tell them the question and leave them to get on with it: they'll frequently give up in despair, without having the foggiest idea where to begin to solve a difficult conundrum.

In this chapter, we'll give you some ideas on how to help your child to work the puzzles out for themselves, with a little guidance from you. It's not giving the game away, merely steering them in the right direction. What seems an impossible task at first sight can be nibbled away at, piece by piece, until the truth is revealed.

As well as working out puzzles designed specifically for that purpose, you can also encourage your children to treat everyday problems as puzzles that need to be solved. In this way, you'll be encouraging them to think laterally, to bring their solving skills to a wider range of issues – and so become more effective thinkers.

Puzzle 1: The Queen's mustard pot

An easy one to start off with. No historical knowledge required – just a small amount of common sense.

The puzzle: *While browsing in an antique shop, you come across a tarnished silver mustard pot. Inscribed on the front is the legend 'Presented to our most loyal subject by Queen Elizabeth I, in the year of Our Lord 1597'. The owner of the shop assures you that the piece is genuine, hence the high price tag. You, however, suspect it to be a forgery. How can you tell?*

Your child may first make all kinds of suppositions: that Queen Elizabeth's reign ended before 1597 (it didn't), that mustard hadn't reached England by that date (it had), that the spelling is too good to be 16th century (it isn't).

They don't need to know anything about Elizabethan history to solve this one. If they're really stuck, ask them what the inscription would have said if the mustard pot had been presented by Queen Victoria. They'll probably come up with a reasonable version of the wording, perhaps even dredging up enough school history to hazard a guess as to a date within Queen Victoria's reign.

What they won't say, of course, is 'presented by Queen Victoria I'. Because she won't be Victoria I until there's been a Victoria II. It's just the same with Elizabeth: it wasn't until the coronation of Queen Elizabeth II that she was referred to as Queen Elizabeth I. In the three and a half centuries before that, she was plain Queen Elizabeth.

Puzzle 2: The helmet problem

This is a tricky one to solve by yourself. There just doesn't seem to be enough to go on. But, as with all the best puzzles, the solution lies in the wording of the question.

The puzzle: *At the beginning of the First World War, soldiers fought in cloth caps or berets. Naturally, there were heavy losses, so they were soon issued with tin helmets instead. However, in the weeks after helmets began to be worn, the field hospitals reported treating a far higher number of casualties with head injuries. Why was this the case?*

Children often approach this puzzle by assuming that there must be a fault with the equipment. Perhaps the helmets weren't as strong as they thought, so they were shot when they put their heads up over the parapet. Perhaps they wore their chin straps too loose, so the helmets were blown off the back of their heads and the straps strangled them.

They have to be assured, at this point, that the helmets were in no way faulty, and that they were being worn and used correctly. They don't need any specialist knowledge of wartime conditions. And no, the soldiers didn't become reckless and foolhardy as a result of wearing what they assumed was adequate protection.

So why were there so many more head injuries?

There weren't. And that's a key point to get across when your child starts to run out of ideas: there were no more head injuries after the helmets were issued than there were before.

Let them stew on this for a while, since it may well be enough to get them thinking along the right lines.

When they get stuck – and they probably will – try repeating the key phrase in the puzzle again: 'Field hospitals reported *treating* a far higher number of casualties with head injuries.' It's the fourth word that gives the game away. Before the helmets were issued, soldiers with head injuries didn't get as far as the hospital.

Puzzle 3: The burning fuses

This one appears baffling at first sight. But it's a straightforward enough problem, and one that most children ought to be able to solve with a little assistance.

The puzzle: *You have two string fuses, of the kind you see attached to round black bombs in cartoons. Each one burns for exactly one hour. They're not of uniform thickness, so may not burn at a constant rate. How can you use these fuses to measure exactly 45 minutes?*

Kids will try to cheat at this one. They'll suggest measuring three-quarters of the way along a fuse, so you must point out that they don't burn in a uniform way. They'll suggest cutting the fuses in half, but the same rule applies.

Eventually, they should realise that if you light one of the fuses at both ends, it will last exactly half an hour. But how does this help? You could try lighting one at both ends to get half an hour, then lighting the other at both ends for another half an hour – but this gets us back to an hour, and we want 45 minutes. So we want the second fuse to last for a shorter time.

Let's say we light the first fuse at both ends, and the other at one end. When the first fuse is completely burnt, half an hour has elapsed. Now what?

The second fuse is now exactly half gone, which means it has half an hour's worth of burning left in it. How can we make this one burn for just 15 minutes? We've already cracked the problem of making a fuse burn twice as fast, so we can apply that solution here. As soon as the first fuse is extinguished, light the second one at the other end as well. The remaining half an hour's worth of fuse will be used up in half the time – 15 minutes. So, in all, we've managed to time 45 minutes.

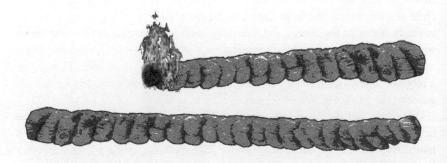

Puzzle 4: The seven trees

This is a puzzle that almost all children fail to get right first time. And they'll continue to make the same mistake each time the puzzle is repeated using different wording – until they finally grasp the point. It's something to do with the way their brains are wired!

The puzzle: *Seven trees are planted in a single line. Each tree is exactly 10 metres from the next. What's the distance between the first tree and the last?*

Most children will immediately answer '70 metres'. Rather than giving them the right answer, simply tell them that their solution is wrong. They'll think about it, multiply seven by ten once more, and come up with the same answer, assuming *you've* got it wrong and can't do basic maths.

It may be helpful, for younger children at least, to draw seven dots in a line on a piece of paper, and get them to count the gaps. Of course, seven trees make six gaps: so the answer is 60 metres, not 70.

Once they get the point, give them the puzzle again over the next few days or weeks, using perhaps ten stones on a beach, or five fence posts, or eleven footballers in a line-up. You'll be surprised at how often they'll get it wrong before they fully grasp the principle!

Puzzle 5: The 100 trees

This is a good puzzle to follow the *seven trees*, as it looks at first sight as if you're simply repeating one they already know. But this is a different case entirely!

The puzzle: *100 trees are planted in a straight line. The distance from the first to the second is 1 metre; from the second to the third is 2 metres; from the third to the fourth is 4 metres, from the fourth to the fifth 8 metres, and so on. The gap between each pair of trees is double the previous one. If you walk from the first tree to the last, which tree are you nearest when you've walked exactly half the total distance?*

Your child may begin here by assuming it's a mathematical task of monstrous proportions, and start adding together 1, 2, 4, 8, 16 and so on. They'll quickly realise that it would take an age to add up all the numbers needed, so reassure them that no such complex maths is necessary. As with all the best puzzles, this one comes down to common sense.

The fact that there are so many trees appears to make this one unmanageable, so ease them into the solution by starting with a smaller number of trees. Let's say there are just five in a row, following the same doubling rule. How far is the total distance between the first and the last? You may need to draw this on paper to help them out.

Once again, they may begin by adding 1, 2, 4, 8 and 16 – the first five multiples. Except, of course, five trees means only four gaps. So all they need to add is the first four numbers, which makes a completely manageable 15. When they're halfway, they've walked 7.5 metres. The gaps between the first four trees (the first three gaps) comes to 7 metres, so they're nearest to the fourth tree.

At this point, they may have that flash of insight that helps them to solve the original puzzle. If not, ask what happens if there are six trees in a row. The total distance is now 31 metres; half that is 15.5 metres; the distance between the first and the fifth is 15 metres, so they're nearest to the fifth tree.

So if halfway between the first and the fifth tree is the fourth, and halfway between the first and the sixth tree is the fifth, what's halfway between the first and the 100th? The answer, of course, is the 99th tree. They'll be seriously impressed with themselves when they figure it out!

Puzzle 6: The chiming clock

Just when they think they've got the hang of the *seven trees* puzzle, it's a good time to give them this one. It looks completely different, but it's exactly the same puzzle.

The puzzle: *A clock takes 5 seconds to chime six o'clock. How long will it take to chime twelve o'clock?*

The immediate response is to double the length of time, giving 10 seconds. That, of course, is the wrong answer: what we're looking for is the time between the first strike and the last. Just like the *seven trees* puzzle, it's a question of counting the gaps. If takes 5 seconds to chime six o'clock, then that's five gaps – one chime per second. So, of course, it takes 11 seconds to chime twelve o'clock.

Puzzle 7: Three cats eating

When maths is involved in a puzzle, it's important to use logic as well as arithmetic to get the right answer. This one baffles most children, despite being fairly straightforward.

The puzzle: *If three cats eat three bowls of food in three days, how much food does one cat eat in one day?*

The first response is generally to divide everything by three, and to come up with the answer: one bowl. But there are too many terms here to be able to do this division so simply; more thought is required. Your first piece of assistance should be to ask them how many bowls of food one cat will eat in three days, which should be enough to get them thinking along the right lines.

If there are three cats, and they eat three bowls in three days, then that's one bowl per cat; so one cat will eat one bowl in the same three days. Which means that one cat will eat one-third of a bowl of food in a single day.

Puzzle 8: Two men walking

Most of the puzzles involve some kind of calculation or logic in order to solve them. But it takes a different kind of logic to realise when a puzzle is, itself, the puzzle. This is a good one to follow the *three cats eating* puzzle.

The puzzle: *It takes one man three hours to walk to London. How long does it take two men to walk to London?*

If they say either six hours or one and a half hours, then they're good at mental arithmetic – but not so good at spotting when they're being fooled. It's still three hours, of course.

Wouldn't it be easier to work this out on paper?

LONDON

Puzzle 9: Three fruit boxes

A very straightforward puzzle, but one that can be hard to visualise. It helps if you have a pen and paper handy to draw a diagram!

The puzzle: *Three boxes of fruit are labelled A (apples), B (bananas) and C (cherries). All the labels on the boxes are wrong. How many boxes do you have to open in order to label them all correctly?*

Rather than simply accepting their initial guess of 'one', 'two' or 'three', get them to explain their reasoning. Having a drawing of three boxes labelled A, B and C in front of you will make it much easier for them to show what they're thinking.

Let's say you open box A, and it has bananas in it. What does that tell us about the contents of box B? Well, it could contain either apples or cherries. But if it had apples in, then box C must contain the cherries, right? Wrong. It can't contain cherries, since all the boxes are labelled incorrectly; so box C must contain the apples, which means the cherries must be in box B.

You can repeat the process with each of the boxes in turn, if you like, but it's probably not necessary since the logic is the same with each box. You only ever have to open one box to be able to label them all correctly.

Puzzle 10: Three coin boxes

This is a good one to follow on from the *three fruit boxes* puzzle, as it takes the problem one step further. It appears to be the same puzzle, but there's an added twist.

The puzzle: *Three boxes of coins are labelled 'Gold', 'Silver', and 'Gold or Silver'. All the labels are wrong: the boxes actually contain gold, silver and bronze coins. How many boxes do you need to open in order to put all the labels right?*

Let's say we open the box labelled Gold, and it contains... no, wait, we don't need to do that. There's a better way of approaching this puzzle, which is to step back and think about it before you start lifting the lids.

Start with the box labelled Gold or Silver. What do we know about that one? Well, obviously, if the label is incorrect, it can't contain either gold or silver coins. So without even opening it, we know that this one must contain the bronze coins.

That should be enough to get them to work out the rest of the problem. Having figured out where the bronze coins are stored, we're left with only the silver and the gold. So what goes where? Clearly, the gold can't be in the box labelled Gold, so it must be in the one labelled silver. And so the silver has to be in the box labelled Gold.

And so we come to the rather surprising solution: we don't have to open any of the boxes in order to put all the labels right.

Puzzle 11: The violinist's dilemma

This is one of those puzzles that seems, at first sight, to be impossible. But the explanation is perfectly rational – although a slight knowledge of Pythagoras certainly helps.

The puzzle: *A violinist is going to perform a concert in a foreign country. He's stopped at the airport check-in desk, and told that he can't board the plane. 'The violin is OK,' says the attendant, 'since it's 40cm long. But that's the maximum dimension of item you're allowed to take on the plane, and your bow is 50cm long. Sorry, you can't take it with you.' The violinist is in despair – he can't play the concert without his bow, and doesn't want to risk putting it in the baggage hold. Eventually, he works out a way to carry it onto the plane legitimately. How's it done?*

It doesn't involve breaking the bow in half, or sliding it down his trouser leg, or any of a dozen ruses the quick-witted child might come up with. So how is it possible?

The Pythagoras solution, mentioned above, is the answer. You'll dimly remember from school maths lessons that if a right-angle triangle has two sides of lengths 3 and 4 units, then the hypotenuse will be 5 units long (since $3^2 + 4^2 = 5^2$). So all the violinist has to do is find a box 30cm by 40cm, and place the bow in it diagonally. Amazing!

Puzzle 12: The age of children

This is the trickiest puzzle in the book, and one which will take some real thought to figure out – for adults as much as for children. Is there enough information to get the solution?

The puzzle: *A man is going from house to house doing market research. He knocks on a door and a woman answers. 'Good morning,' says the man. 'I wonder if you can tell me how many children you have?' 'Three,' answers the woman. 'And how old are they?' The woman, being rather mischievous, tells him: 'The product of their ages is*

36.' [That is, you get 36 if you multiply all their ages together.] 'That doesn't give me the answer,' says the man. The woman replies: 'The sum of their ages [that is, if you add them all together] is the same as the number of the house next door.' The man goes to look at the neighbour's house, then comes back with a despondent look on his face. 'That still doesn't tell me,' he says. The woman gives him one final clue: 'The oldest plays the piano.' Now the researcher can work out the children's ages exactly. How does he know?

At first glance, it looks as if we don't have anything like enough information here. For one thing, the researcher may know the number of the house next door, but we don't. And what possible difference can it make if the oldest plays the piano?

The only solution is to take each piece of information in turn. We know that the product of the children's ages is 36; so we can begin by working out all the permutations of three children that multiply together to make 36. Write them in columns:

36	18	12	9	9	6	6	4
1	2	3	4	2	6	3	3
1	1	1	1	2	1	2	3

Next, we know that the sum of the ages is equal to the number on the house next door. Well, we don't know that number, but let's add up all the sums:

36	18	12	9	9	6	6	4
1	2	3	4	2	6	3	3
1	1	1	1	2	1	2	3
38	21	16	14	13	13	11	10

We know that, even knowing the sum of the ages, this information wasn't enough to give the researcher the ages of the children. In order for there still to be some doubt, this means that the number on the house next door must be 13, as there are two possible solutions with this sum. So the ages of the children is either 9, 2 and 2, or 6, 6 and 1.

And the final piece of information? The eldest plays the piano. If they were 6, 6 and 2, there would be two older twins: but 'the oldest' indicates a single person. So the children have to be aged 9, 2 and 2.

Simple? Far from it. But you'll look most impressive to your kids when you show them how it's worked out!

Puzzle 13: The hungry bookworm

This one seems, at first sight, like a straightforward problem of addition. And so it is: but you need to use a little logic before you begin adding.

The puzzle: *Three volumes of an encyclopaedia are arranged in order on a shelf. The pages of each book are each 30mm thick, and each hard cover is 5mm thick. A bookworm eats its way from the first page of volume 1 to the last page of volume 3. How far does it travel?*

Simple, your child thinks. Each book is 30mm for the pages, plus 5mm for each cover. Add them up, and you get a thickness of 40mm for each book. There are three books, so that makes 120mm in total. No, hang on: the worm doesn't go

through the first cover, or the last. So it's 110mm.

Except that it isn't. Tell them they've got the answer wrong, and that they should go and look at a book on a shelf to see why.

The encyclopaedias are arranged in order. Where's the first page of volume 1? On the *right* hand side of the book as you look at the spine. And the last page of volume 3 is on the *left* hand side of the book.

So to eat from the first page of volume 1 to the last page of volume 3, the bookworm only has to eat through one cover of volume one (5mm); then the whole of volume 2 (40mm); then one cover of volume 3 (5mm). Which makes 50mm in all.

Puzzle 14: Manhole covers

With all the made-up puzzles, it's good to pose some questions that relate to real life every now and again. This one's a good example.

The puzzle: *Why are manhole covers usually round?*

You'll get all sorts of answers to this one: you should point out that there's a distinct advantage in them being round, rather than rectangular, or triangular, or any other shape. Try to get them to think about the special properties of round things.

The answer, of course, is that a round cover can never fall down the hole from which it has been lifted. Just about every other shape can.

Puzzle 15: The tennis tournament

Even kids who are a whiz at mental arithmetic will find this one daunting on first sight. But you have to reassure them that maths really has nothing to do with it: all you need is a bit of logic.

The puzzle: *128 people take part in a knockout tennis tournament. Each player drops out as soon as they lose a match. How many matches are played in total?*

Well, this shouldn't be too complicated. 128 is double 64, which is double 32, which is double 16, which is double 8, and so on, so all we have to work out is two multiplied by itself enough times to make…

No, stop right there. As we said, there's really no mathematics involved. Look at it from a logical point of view. How many outright winners are there? Just the one. So how many losers? Well, it has to be 127. And since each player can lose only one match, that means there must have been 127 matches in all. Easy when you think about it!

Puzzle 16: Bags of gold

Another puzzle that looks more complicated than it really is. There's a neat solution here that may take a while to arrive at.

The puzzle: *You have five bags full of gold coins (lucky you!). Although they look identical, the coins in four of the bags weigh 10 grammes each, while those in one of the bags weigh 11 grammes. You also have an accurate set of scales that shows the weight placed upon it. How do you work out which bag holds the heavier coins?*

The first thing to explain here is that you only need one weighing in order to find which bag holds the heavy coins. So how is it done?

Here's the solution: tell your kids to take one coin from bag 1, two from bag 2, three from bag 3, and so on. We'll have 15 coins altogether (1+2+3+4+5). But how does this help?

If they all weighed 10 grammes, the total weight would be 150 grammes. Of course, because of the heavier coins, the total will be slightly more than that. How much more, exactly?

And this will give us the answer. If the total is 2 grammes heavier, then there must be two oversized coins – which means bag 2 contains them. If it's 4 grammes overweight, then bag 4 holds the heavier coins. Simple, when you know how!

Puzzle 17: Not enough time

There's a bit of maths involved in this one. Not a lot, but enough to get them thinking. The answer, however, owes more to logic than mathematics.

The puzzle: *James insists that he does not have enough time to go to school more than 17 days a year. He comes to this conclusion based on the following list that he put together.*

Activity	Number of days per year
Sleep (8 hours a day)	122
Meals (2 hours a day)	31
Weekends	104
School holidays	60
TV & play time (2 hours a day)	31
Total	348

Inspired by the list, James claims he has only 17 days left in the year for school. What's wrong with his thinking?

Get a calculator out, if you like, to check James's sums – but you'll find they're all correct. So where has he gone wrong? It all appears to make sense!

The problem is that James's categories overlap. For example, he's counted 60 days for holidays, during which time he will both eat and sleep, activities that he has already counted separately. These 60 days also include weekends, another category that he has already counted separately. He should not count the same periods of time more than once. Similarly, his weekend counting includes sleeping time, and so on.

Puzzle 18: Running the race

The puzzle: *You're running a race to a distant landmark and back. On the way there, you run at 10 miles per hour. On the way back, you're tired, so only run at 5 miles per hour. What's your average speed over the whole race?*

You might be tempted to say 7.5 miles per hour, which seems logical. But it's not the right answer. Let's imagine this is a 20 mile race. The first 10 miles take one hour; the second ten miles take two hours.

So you've run 20 miles in three hours in all, which makes an average speed of $6\frac{2}{3}$ miles per hour – irrespective of the length of the race.

Quickfire puzzles

Quickfire 1: *What's wrong with these sentences?*

1. No one goes to that restaurant these days because it's too crowded.
2. If you can't read this sign, ask for help.
3. Stay away from the water until you've learned how to swim.

Answers: 1. If no one goes, how can it be crowded? 2. If you can't read, how do you know what it tells you to do? 3. You can't learn how to swim unless you go in the water.

Quickfire 2: *Where would you be if, when you move forward it is summer, backwards and it's winter, right and it's July 1st, left and it's July 2nd?*

Answer: Where the equator meets the International Dateline, facing north.

Quickfire 3: *What are the most northerly, southerly, westerly and easterly states of the USA?*

Answer: Alaska, Hawaii, Alaska and… Alaska. That's right. The Aleutian Islands, part of the state of Alaska, cross the International Dateline and so are both the furthest west *and* east you can go in the United States.

Quickfire 4: *If a friend tells you he's hidden a twenty pound note in a boring dictionary between pages 813 and 814, would you believe him?*

Answer: No, because odd page numbers are on the right hand side of every book and even on the left, which means there is nothing between 813 and 814. They are two sides of the same piece of paper.

Quickfire 5: *What's the only fruit to have its seeds on the outside?*

Answer: A strawberry.

Quickfire 6: *A sundial is the timepiece with the fewest number of moving parts. What is the timepiece with the greatest number of moving parts?*

Answer: An hourglass, which has thousands of moving grains of sand.

The chequerboard illusion

Here's our Dad devising a new board game. All the squares except two have counters on them. The two squares that *don't* contain counters are exactly the same colour. Don't believe us? Punch a couple of holes in a sheet of paper and place it on top, so you can see only those two squares through the holes. It's amazing how the eye is deceived!

That's the last time I buy a cube from IKEA

The impossible cube

This wooden cube has got into a tangle, and Dad's trying to sort it out. Is it possible, do you think? Or is our valiant would-be fixer fighting a losing battle?

9 Stuff and nonsense

THERE ARE MANY THINGS that mark out a great Dad. The ability to fix things, to entertain kids, to play football in the park – these are all essential skills, as we'd be the first to admit. But a Dad is also expected to know stuff that no one else does: not just general information, but stuff so obscure your kids will wonder how you ever came to know it all.

What's the chance of being struck by lightning? What colour is a polar bear? When were tea bags invented? All facts a Dad needs at his fingertips. The opportunities for showing off your intricate knowledge of the bizarre, the wonderful and the downright homely are endless. Whether in a restaurant, on a car journey, in the home or out and about on a shopping trip, you should be able to amaze and entertain your kids with a wealth of information.

Not everything you tell your kids needs to be informative, or even true. So we've added a selection of really, *really* silly jokes and riddles to keep you going.

Fascinating facts

Information is power, we're told. That may or may not be the case with these tasty morsels: but as far as our researches can tell, they're all 100 per cent true.

Babies are born without kneecaps. The knees don't show up on X-rays, as they're made of cartilage; they only turn into bone at the age of around three in girls and five in boys.

Pigs can't look at the sky. They just aren't physically able to bend their necks back far enough. Oh, and they can't fly, either.

Branwell Brontë died standing up. The brother (left) of novelists Charlotte, Emily and Anne contracted tuberculosis, and met his untimely end standing up while leaning against a mantelpiece, simply in order to prove that it could be done.

The Mona Lisa once hung on the wall of Napoleon's bedroom. When it was stolen from the Louvre in 1911, the artist Pablo Picasso was taken for questioning by the police. It turned out to have been stolen by a thief who commissioned a well-known forger to make several copies that he could sell to collectors.

The average lifespan of a rat is 18 months. But they breed so quickly that in that time they could have over a million descendants.

Tsar Nicholas's finger was chopped off in 2001. Legend has it that when the Tsar sketched the route of the Trans-Siberian Railway from Moscow to St Petersburg, he drew a straight line with a ruler on the map – but his finger got in the way, which produced a kink in the line. The engineers faithfully followed his instructions, constructing a 17 kilometre detour near the town of Novgorod. 150 years later, the 'kink' was removed and the line put straight.

Dolphins sleep with one eye open. Sharks, on the other hand, don't find fish by looking for them: they listen for their heartbeats.

The first couple to be shown in bed together on American TV were Fred and Wilma Flintstone.

The average Frenchman eats 500 snails a year. Snails themselves, however, can sleep for three years without eating. The world's largest exporter of frogs' legs is Japan.

The most popular pizza topping in the United States is pepperoni – served on over half of all pizzas sold. In India, favourite toppings include pickled ginger and minced mutton.

If you shave a tiger, the skin underneath will be striped. Best not to try this at home, though.

Jesus Christ is the 13th greatest American of all time, according to a recent poll. Ronald Reagan came first. Another poll revealed that 12 per cent of Americans think Joan of Arc was married to Noah.

Australian banknotes are made of plastic. The first polypropylene polymer note was made in Australia 1988, and contained a transparent window in which an image of Captain James Cook appeared. Today, all banknotes in Australia are made of the same material.

Venus is the only planet which rotates clockwise. All the other planets in the solar system rotate anticlockwise, relative to the Sun, except Uranus, which has tilted so far on its axis that it rolls on its side.

Polar bears are actually black. At least, that's the colour of their skin, since it absorbs more heat that way. Their fur, however, isn't white. It's transparent.

There is no ozone at the seaside. The smell, which happens to be similar to that of ozone, is actually rotting seaweed.

The .tv domain name is owned by Tuvalu. The tiny island in the Pacific has an area of just ten square miles, and a population of under 12,000. No point on the island is more than five metres above sea level, and they're seriously worried about global warming.

Every cubic mile of seawater contains about 25 tons of gold. The trouble is, no-one has yet found a cost-effective way of extracting it. So don't add a filtration plant to your seaside kit just yet. A cubic mile is actually an awful lot of water – the equivalent of over one and a half million Olympic sized swimming pools.

The Hawaiian alphabet has only 13 letters – A, E, I, O, U, H, K, L, M, N, P, W and a type of apostrophe, called 'okina'. Chinese script, on the other hand, has more than 40,000 characters.

Planespotting

So many summer afternoons are ruined – or enhanced, depending on your point of view – by the constant drone of planes flying overhead. Rather than simply cursing them for spoiling your peace and quiet, here's your chance to show your limitless knowledge by pointing out exactly what they are.

These are the planes you'll most often see flying over Britain.

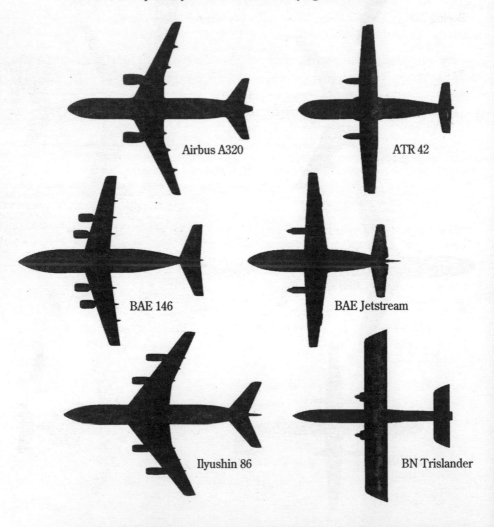

Airbus A320

ATR 42

BAE 146

BAE Jetstream

Ilyushin 86

BN Trislander

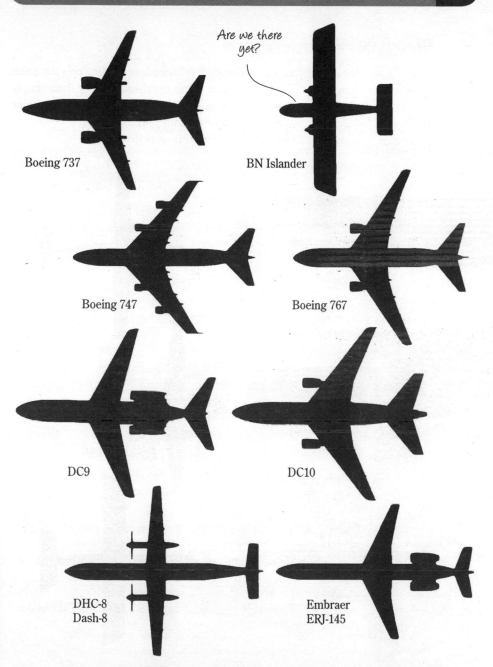

Names of the trade

We're all familiar with the household names of the products we use every day. But where did these names – and the products themselves – come from? A great opportunity to show off to your kids every time one crops up!

Rolls-Royce had a succession of cars with airy-fairy names such as Silver Ghost, Silver Wraith and Silver Phantom. Then they came up with 'Silver Mist' which seemed fine, until somebody pointed out that 'Mist' is the German name for 'manure'. The car became the 'Silver Shadow' instead.

The name **Frisbee** comes from the pie-tins that people discovered had aerodynamic properties when they were thrown. These came from the Frisbie Bakery in Connecticut, North America. The first Frisbee as such came out in 1957, made by the Wham-O Manufacturing Company in California.

Hoover: Compact electric vacuum cleaners were invented not by a Mr Hoover but by J. Murray Spangler, a department store caretaker who thought that the carpet sweeper he was told to use was making his asthma worse. William Henry Hoover was the businessman who bought the rights from him.

The principle behind it, though, had been adopted earlier by the British engineer H. Cecil Booth. He first demonstrated the idea by putting a handkerchief on a chair and sucking it, noting the dirt that collected on the other side. However, his devices were drawn by horses and originally oil-fired, and pipes had to be run into the building to be cleaned – not the most practical of methods.

Jelly Babies: Initially produced by Bassett's in Sheffield in 1919, they were originally called 'Peace Babies', as the First World War had just ended. They were known by that name right up to 1953 when they became Jelly Babies. The white stuff on the outside is edible starch, which was originally used to stop the sweets sticking in the old wooden moulds. It's still added because customers grew to like it.

Black jelly babies are made from leftover bits of all the other colours. More than a billion are produced every year, and they have names: Brilliant is red, Bubbles is yellow, Bonny is pink, Bigheart is black, Boofuls is green and Bumper is orange.

WD-40: The great lubricating spray that has so many uses, stands for 'Water Displacement, 40th Attempt'. It was invented as a way of preventing corrosion by keeping water at bay and was first used on the outside of Atlas missiles to stop them rusting.

On sale since 1958 and produced by what was then called The Rocket Chemical Company, it has many unconventional uses, such as removing chewing gum from shoes, cleaning computer mice and keyboards, getting rid of spray snow after Christmas, spraying on fishing bait to cover up the smell of human hands and, perhaps most useful of all, freeing a tongue that has become stuck to metal in freezing weather.

Mr Kipling's Cakes: There never was a Mr Kipling. His name was conjured up in the 1960s as a supposed 'master baker', simply because it sounded mellifluous and traditional.

Subbuteo: Peer Adolph, who invented this football game in 1947, wanted to call it 'The Hobby', after the breed of falcon. But he wasn't allowed to use such an all-embracing name, so instead he named it after the falcon's Latin name *Falco subbuteo subbuteo*.

Crisps: The invention of crisps was a complete accident. In 1853 George Crum, a Native American chef at Moon's Lake House in Saratoga Springs in New York became irritated by a fussy diner who claimed that the chips he made were too thick and not salty enough.

After he sent them back a second time, Crum wanted to teach the customer a lesson. So he made the chips as thin as he possibly could and poured oodles of salt over them, reckoning the guy would never be able to eat them with a fork and would hate the taste. Instead, the diner loved them. And so the crisp was born.

Post-it notes: The adhesive on Post-it notes, just sticky enough but not so sticky it damages whatever it's attached to, was invented at 3M back in 1959 by Dr Spence Silver. Unfortunately, Dr Silver had been trying to produce a strong adhesive, so his formula was forgotten about.

21 years later another 3M employee, Art Fry, was trying to find a bookmark that would keep his place in his hymn book when he sang with his church choir. He experimented with Dr Silver's formula and came up with the Post-it note.

Initially, his bosses couldn't see the point. So Fry gave some secretaries at the company the first trial blocks of Post-it notes to see what they'd use them for. They proved so popular that the order was given to manufacture what has since become one of the most popular stationery products ever, with a billion sold. As an employee of 3M, however, Art Fry didn't become rich as a result.

How loud is it?

Scientists will tell you that it means nothing to describe a noise as being so many decibels (named in honour of Alexander Graham Bell, inventor of the telephone). But then scientists say it isn't possible to travel faster than the speed of light and that we'll never have transporter beams, so they're just spoilsports.

Technically, a decibel is a unit of comparison rather than an absolute measure. But decibels are almost always related to the quietest sound that somebody with normal hearing can detect.

Decibels are measured on a logarithmic scale so that 20db, for instance, isn't double 10db but 10 times as loud, while 30db is 100 times as loud. It's also interesting to point out that 0db isn't absolute silence: it's just the point below which people can't hear.

Bizarrely, a nuclear submarine has audio detection equipment so sensitive that it can detect prawns chewing on food from 100 metres away, a sound level that is apparently –80db. By way of comparison, somebody talking 20 miles away would be –30db.

0db	**20db**	**40db**	**60db**	**70db**	**75db**	**90db**
Lowest level of human audibility	A soft whisper, rustling leaves	Suburban street with no traffic	Background music in a restaurant, normal conversation	Busy traffic, a noisy restaurant, noise inside a jet plane	Vacuum cleaner	Orchestra playing at its loudest heard from front row

If anybody says it's quiet enough to hear a pin drop, you can tell them that would measure 15db, assuming it was a metre away falling from a height of one centimetre (and not onto a cushion).

Sudden loud noises may startle but our ears are sensitive instruments, and if noise is continuous our hearing can be permanently damaged. Noise above 85db 8 hours a day will eventually harm hearing as will 15 minutes at 115db and 2 minutes at 130. MP3 players can often play above 115db, and while iPods are limited in Europe to 100db, that can still cause permanent problems if listened to at full volume for extended periods, particularly as the earbud style of headphones that intrude into the ear are noisier than the conventional sort. If you listen while travelling and turn the music up to drown out the noise of a busy street or a train, it can be difficult to tell just how loud the sound really is.

Experts recommend a 60/60 rule, listening for no more than an hour at a time at 60 per cent of maximum volume. Perhaps it's better to endure loud music coming from your kids' rooms than have them saying, 'Pardon, dad', every time you try talking to them in ten years' time.

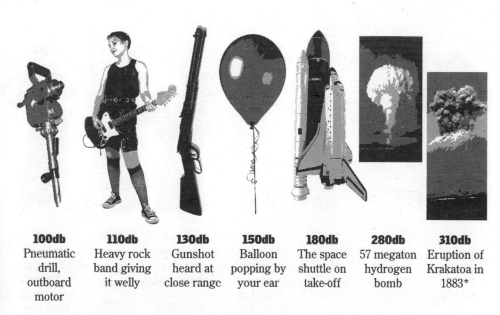

100db	**110db**	**130db**	**150db**	**180db**	**280db**	**310db**
Pneumatic drill, outboard motor	Heavy rock band giving it welly	Gunshot heard at close range	Balloon popping by your ear	The space shuttle on take-off	57 megaton hydrogen bomb	Eruption of Krakatoa in 1883*

heard 3,000 miles away, shattered concrete 30 centimetres thick 300 miles away

When did they start eating...

Popcorn, 3–2000 BC
Ancient popping corn was discovered in New Mexico during an archaeological dig in in 1948.

Chewing gum, 1869
William Semple filed the first patent on chewing gum, though the Ancient Greeks chewed resin from the mastic tree.

Corn Flakes, 1894
Dr John Harvey Kellogg, a Seventh-Day Adventist who ran the Battle Creek Sanitarium, insisted on a vegetarian regimen that forbade booze, caffeine, tobacco or sex. Corn flakes, invented by accident, were thought to lower the sex drive and were served with milk and marshmallows.

Baked beans, 1890s
In Britain, where baked beans were introduced in 1904, beans are usually associated with Heinz, and Henry J. Heinz first came up with his baked beans in tomato sauce in Pittsburgh in 1895. However, the top baked bean producer in America is actually Bush's and even Heinz beans in the US are very different to the UK, being darker, mushier and much more sugary. In some places beans are sweetened with maple syrup or have mustard added.

Ice-cream cone, 1904
The cone first came to the public's attention at the St Louis Fair of 1904 where it's said that a pastry maker helped out an ice-cream salesman who had run out of dishes. But there are several rival claims.

Tea bag, 1904
The first tea bags, made from hand-sewn muslin bags, appeared in 1904 and were sold by Thomas Sullivan of New York. Tea connoisseurs despise tea bags for containing low grade, dusty tea, known as 'floor sweepings', that make the tea taste harsher than using leaves in a pot.

Instant coffee, 1909
Although invented by Japanese scientist Satori Kato in Chicago in 1901, instant coffee wasn't actually available commercially until Nescafé was launched by Nestlé in Switzerland, in 1938.

Frozen food, 1925
On a trip to the Arctic, Clarence Birdseye (his real name!) noticed that fish that froze quickly still tasted fresh when it was defrosted months later. In 1925 he developed a commercial freezer which kick-started the frozen foods industry.

Sliced bread, 1928

If something's 'the best thing since sliced bread' then that really means since 7 July 1928, which is when the Chillicothe Baking Company of Missouri first produced 'Kleen Maid Sliced Bread' from their new slicing machine. It took a little while, though, to work out how to wrap the loaves and it wasn't until 1930 that pre-sliced 'Wonder Bread' was sold throughout the USA and in the UK.

Campbell's tomato soup, 1932

Although tomato soup exists before this, it was in 1932 that Campbell's first produced their tomato soup, made even more famous by Andy Warhol.

Shopping trolley, 1937

Apparently basing it on the traditional design of a folding wooden chair, Sylvan Goldman came up with the first trolley. It looked like a folding chair on wheels with one basket where the seat would be and another higher up and further back. A year later, they added a holder for young children as customers were simply putting their kids in the baskets, which was dangerous as the early trolleys had a tendency to fold up unexpectedly.

Initially customers wouldn't use them. Men thought others would think they were too weak to carry baskets while they reminded women of pushing baby carriages. He had to employ fake customers to push them around before they took off.

Fish fingers, 1946

Frozen 'fish sticks' were apparently first conjured up by Edward Piszek of Philadelphia, although the American firm Gorton's claim they were there first. In the UK, however, the introduction of 'fish fingers' was an error. They were

originally made of herring, a fish the British didn't really like and called 'herring savouries'. To show just how tasty they were, bland cod sticks were made to compare them with but the British, being suitably perverse, preferred the cod version.

Chicken nugget, 1950s

Contrary to popular opinion, it wasn't McDonald's that came up with Jamie Oliver's least favourite food, it was food science professor Robert Baker of Cornell University. He worked out how to form chicken bits (comprising skin, muscle tissue and reconstituted meat) into any shape before being coated with breadcrumbs before cooking. Sadly for him, he didn't patent his findings.

What's the chance of...

Dying from a plane falling on you . . . . 1 in 25,000,000*

Dying from a lightning strike . . . . 1 in 18,700,000*

Dying from motorcycle racing. . . . . 1 in 1,100**

Dying from mountain climbing . . . . 1 in 1,750**

Dying from smoking 10 cigarettes a day . . . . 1 in 200**

Dying from having a meteorite fall on you. . . . . 1 in 1,000,000,000,000*

Dying from a road accident . . . . 1 in 16,800*

Dying from playing football . . . . 1 in 50,000**

Dying in a rail accident. . . . . 1 in 1,000,000*

Dying from a nuclear power accident. . . . . 1 in 10,000,000*

Being killed by a tree in a public space . . . . 1 in 20,000,000*

Drowning in the bath . . . . 1 in 685,000*

Being murdered . . . . 1 in 100,000*

Dying on a fairground ride. . . . . 1 in 834,000,000 rides

Dying while scuba diving. . . . . 1 in 200,000 dives

Dying while rock climbing. . . . . 1 in 320,000 climbs

Dying while hang-gliding. . . . . 1 in 116,000 flights

Having a serious fire at home . . . . 1 in 160*

Seriously injuring yourself using exercise equipment . . . . 1 in 400**

Having an accident on a fairground ride . . . . 1 in 2,326,000 rides

Finding that the next person you meet
is born on exactly the same day as you . . . . 1 in 25,000

Getting three balls in the National Lottery . . . . 1 in 11

Winning the National Lottery jackpot . . . . 1 in 14,000,000

*   per year
** but only if you race motorcycles, climb mountains, smoke, play football or use
    exercise equipment

Sources: Royal Society of Chemistry, HSE, National Statistics

The cloudspotter's guide

Sometimes they're fluffy and look like elephants or floating castles. Seen from above in glorious sunshine from a plane window, they look like beautifully-lit cotton wool. But you might need to know a little more about clouds if you are to head off inquisitive questions, particularly as the beasties are so important to our weather.

All clouds are made up of billions of tiny droplets of ice or water, each droplet so tiny (1/100 of a millimetre) and light that they float on air. Every cubic metre of air contains 100 million droplets. If a child wants to know what it is like being in a cloud, take them out next time it is foggy, for fog is, in fact, simply cloud that is touching the ground.

A cloud is formed when the water vapour in the air cools and condenses into visible water droplets or ice crystals. It is the same process that results in condensation on windows and usually happens when warm air rises. Air might be forced to rise up over hills or mountains. It might rise because the ground has been heated by the sun, creating thermals that birds and gliders like to ride. Or a body of warm air might meet a mass of cold, denser air and be forced up, which is called a 'front'.

What are contrails?

A shortening of 'condensation trails', these are composed of water vapour produced by the engines of high-flying jets that have condensed in the atmosphere where it is 30 degrees below zero. Although they aren't really clouds, these trails of ice crystals may be visible for some time and in some cases can spread and become the basis of cirrus clouds.

Identifying clouds

Although it can be fun trying to find shapes or faces in clouds, scientists prefer to be a little more precise. Back in 1803, Luke Howard, a chemist of the 'something for the weekend?' variety and a keen amateur meteorologist, came up with the system still used today. Using Latin for his definitions, he said that all clouds were either cumulus – heaped up and fluffy, stratus – in a layer, cirrus – wispy like threads or filaments or nimbus – Latin for 'get out your brolly'.

There are ten main cloud types, divided into three layers of height, depending on where the base of the cloud is. See the following pages for a full description of each one.

Low level clouds – below 1 mile

Cumulus
The white, fluffy cloud kids love drawing. May bring showers but most often associated with sunny spells.

Cumulonimbus
White on top with a dark underside, like a cumulus which goes much higher and becomes less distinct, sometimes with an anvil shape at the top. This towering storm cloud produces heavy showers at the least and perhaps hail and thunder.

Stratocumulus
Fluffy cloud which resembles stretched-out cumulus and might be in layers or patches. Common in the UK in the colder months, it may produce light rain or snow but is more likely indicative of dry and dull weather.

Stratus
A low-level, grey layer of cloud. If there's nothing above it, you might just be able to see the sun through it but don't bet on it. On higher ground it's known as hill fog. At lower levels, ordinary fog that lifts may turn into stratus. Stratus might produce drizzle.

Medium level clouds – 1 to 3 miles

Altocumulus
White or grey with shading, like patches or sheets of medium-height cumulus. Might produce a shower but sunny periods are more likely.

Altostratus
A sheet of grey or bluish cloud without texture covering much of the sky. Altostratus will probably produce light rain or snow.

Nimbostratus
A thick, dark grey, layered rain cloud covering most or all of the sky and obscuring the sun. Will make rain or snow, possibly heavy.

High level clouds – over 3 miles

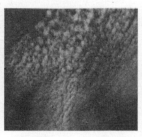

Cirrus
High, wispy, white cloud composed of ice crystals in long streaks or filaments, often described as 'mares' tails'. Cirrus is an indication of bad weather on the way.

Cirrocumulus
Often called a 'mackerel sky', these high-level clouds are made of ice crystals. The individual clusters will appear the width of your finger at arm's length. Indicative of unsettled weather.

Cirrostratus
Layered white cloud made of ice crystals, thin enough for the sun to cast shadows. Will sometimes produce haloes around the sun or the moon. Showers or rain could be on the way.

Timeline of inventions

When did they think of that? Not an exhaustive list, but it includes many of the inventions your kids are likely to ask you about.

1590 Microscope
Zacharias Janssen

1593 Water thermometer
Galileo

1608 Telescope
Hans Lippershey

1643 Barometer
Evangelista Torricelli

1656 Pendulum clock
Christiaan Huygens

1668 Reflecting telescope
Isaac Newton

1700 Piano
Bartolomeo Cristofori

1705 Steam engine
Thomas Newcomen

1714 Mercury thermometer
Daniel Fahrenheit

1764 Bifocal lens
Benjamin Franklin

1783 Balloon
The Montgolfier brothers

1800 Electric battery
Alessandro Volta

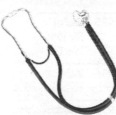

1816 Stethoscope
René-Théophile-Hyacinthe Laënnec

1821 Electric motor
Michael Faraday

1827 Friction match
John Walker

1830 Sewing machine
Barthélemy Thimonnier

1831 Dynamo
Michael Faraday

1835 Pistol
Samuel Colt

1839 Electrical telegraph
Cooke & Wheatstone

1840 Postage stamps
Rowland Hill

1840 Calculator
Charles Babbage

1844 Safety matches
Gustaf Pasch

1849 Safety pin
Walter Hunt

1852 Safety lift
Elisha Otis

1853 Hypodermic syringe
Alexander Wood

1861 Machine gun
Richard Gatling

1862 Pedal bicycle
Pierre Lallenent

1867 Dynamite
Alfred Nobel

1876 Telephone
Alexander Graham Bell & E. Gray

| 1876 | **Microphone** Emile Berliner |
| 1877 | **Phonograph** Thomas Edison |

I've had a great idea

1879	**Electric light** Joseph Swan
1885	**Automobile** Karl Benz
1887	**Pneumatic rubber tyre** J. B. Dunlop

1887	**Gramophone** Emile Berliner
1888	**Roll film camera** George Eastman
1891	**Glider** Otto Lilienthal
1892	**Vacuum flask** James Dewar
1893	**Motion pictures** Thomas Edison
1895	**X-ray** Wilhelm Röntgen

1896	**Radio** Marchese Marconi
1903	**Aeroplane** Wright brothers
1913	**Zip fastener** Gideon Sundback
1926	**Television** John Logie Baird
1928	**Penicillin** Sir Alexander Fleming
1930	**Jet engine** Sir Frank Whittle
1934	**Cats' eyes** Percy Shaw
1935	**Radar** Sir Robert Watson-Watt
1936	**Helicopter** Heinrich Focke
1938	**Photocopier** Chester Carlson
1938	**Ballpoint pen** Laszlo Bíró

1945	**Microwave oven** Percy Spencer
1951	**Superglue** Harry Coover
1954	**Solar battery** Bell Laboratory

| 1955 | **Hovercraft** Christopher Cockerell |

1956	**Videotape** Charles Ginsberg & Ray Dolby
1959	**Integrated circuit** Jack Kilby
1960	**Laser** Theodore Maiman

1964	**Computer mouse** Douglas Engelbart
1968	**LCD display** George Heilmeier
1971	**Pocket calculator** Sharp
1971	**Microprocessor** Hoff & Faggin
1977	**Home computer** Jobs & Wozniak
1979	**Walkman stereo** Akio Morita
1982	**Compact disc** Philips & Sony
1990	**World Wide Web** Tim Berners-Lee

Doctors, bars and other jokes

'Doctor, Doctor, I swallowed a bone.'
'Are you choking?'
'No, I really did.'

'Doctor, Doctor, I've got wind! Can you give me something?'
'Of course. Here's a kite.'

'Doctor, Doctor, I think I'm suffering from Déjà vu!'
'Didn't I see you yesterday?'

'Doctor, Doctor, my son has swallowed my pen. What should I do?'
'Use a pencil.'

'Doctor, Doctor, I think I'm a bell.'
'Take these, and if it doesn't help give me a ring.'

'Doctor, Doctor, I get a pain in my eye every time I drink coffee.'
'Try taking the teaspoon out.'

'Doctor, Doctor, I've lost my memory.'
'When did this happen?'
'When did what happen?'

'Doctor, Doctor, I feel like a pair of curtains.'
'Pull yourself together.'

Why did the banana go to the doctors? Because he wasn't pealing well.

A man walks into a bar. 'Ouch!'

William Shakespeare walks into a bar. 'Out!' orders the barman. 'You're bard.'

A white horse walks into a pub. The barman says, 'That's funny, this pub is named after you.'
The white horse says, 'What? William?'

A skeleton walks into a bar, and orders a beer and a mop.

A sandwich walks into a bar and asks for a drink. The barman says, 'I'm sorry, but we don't serve food in here.'

A man walks into a bar, with a newt on his shoulder and says, 'A beer for me and an orange juice for Tiny here.'
'Why do you call him Tiny?'
'Because he's my newt.'

An Englishman, an Irishman and a Scotsman walk into a bar. 'What is this?' asks the barman, 'some sort of joke?'

'Mummy, Mummy can we have a dog for Christmas?'
'No, we'll have turkey like everyone else!'

Did you hear about the magic tractor? It turned into a field.

'What a terrible day. I got pneumonia, then appendicitis, then tonsillitis.'
'You poor thing.'
'Yup, it's the hardest spelling test ever.'

A policeman stops a car packed full of penguins. The driver says he found them running around by the side of the road. 'You should take them to the zoo,' says the policeman.
The following day, at the same spot, he sees the same guy driving by with his car full of penguins again. He orders the man to stop. 'I thought I told you to take them to the zoo.'
'I did,' says the man. 'They had so much fun we're going to the beach today.'

What did Tarzan say when he saw a herd of elephants coming over a hill? 'Here come the elephants.'

What did Tarzan say when he saw a herd of elephants coming over the hill wearing sunglasses? Nothing. He didn't recognise them.

How do you tell when you are sharing your bed with an elephant? He has 'E' embroidered on his pyjamas.

Do you want me to tell you the joke about butter? I'd better not. You'd only spread it.

Do you want to hear a joke about the bed? I haven't made it up yet.

Did you hear about the man who drowned in a bowl of muesli? He was pulled under by a strong currant.

Did you hear about the three eggs? Two bad.

Have I told you the joke about the pencil? I'd better not, you won't get the point.

Knock. knock.
Donkheap.
Donkheap who?

Knock, knock
Who's there?
Biggish.
Biggish who?
No thanks, I just bought one.

A three-year-old put his shoes on by himself. His mother looked and said, 'Your shoes are on the wrong feet.'
'Don't be silly, Mum. They're the only feet I've got.'

The commander of a firing squad asks a man about to be shot for his last request. 'I'd like to sing a song,' he says. His request is granted. 'A million green bottles, standing on the wall...'

'Oh Mum, don't make me go to school today. I hate it.'
'You have to, son. For a start, you're 45. Secondly, you're the headmaster.'

Silly riddles

Two men jump into a lake but only one gets wet hair. How come?
One of them was bald.

Where do you find a dog with no legs?
Exactly where you left it.

What has a bottom at the top?
Your legs.

What part of the fish weighs the most?
The scales.

What's the difference between roast beef and pea soup?
Anyone can roast beef.

What do you call an elephant in space?
Lost.

What's green and wears oven gloves?
A cooking apple.

What did the dragon say when he saw St George in his armour?
'Oh no, not tinned food again.'

If Isambard Kingdom Brunel were alive today, what would he be most famous for?
Being the oldest person alive.

What has four wheels and flies?
A dustbin lorry.

Why did the hedgehog cross the road?
To see his flat mate.

How do you cook toast in the jungle?
Under the gorilla.

Why do the French like snails?
Because they don't like fast food.

What goes up, but never comes down?
Your age.

Why does Peter Pan always fly?
Because he can 'Neverland'.

What gets wetter as it dries?
A towel.

What is the similarity between a monkey and a bicycle?
They both have wheels, except for the monkey.

What's the best way to see flying saucers?
Insult the waiter.

How many Spaniards does it take to change a lightbulb?
Just Juan.

What's green, is fuzzy, has four legs, and could kill you if it fell from a tree?
A snooker table.

Where do lions like to shop?
At a jungle sale.

What goes 'Oooohhhhh. Oooohhhh'?
A cow with no lips.

What goes 'Aaaa. Aaaa'?
A sheep with no lips.

Why did the dinosaur cross the road?
Because chickens hadn't yet been invented.

What's slow and sad?
Depressed treacle.

What's red and smells like blue paint?
Red paint.

What do you call a donkey with three legs?
Wonky.

What's green and has wheels?
Grass. I was joking about the wheels.

What's yellow and fills the field with music?
Popcorn.

What do you call a piece of wood with nothing to do?
Board.

What do you call a dinosaur with one eye?
Doyouthinkhesaurus.

Why did the teacher take a ruler to bed with him?
To see how long he could sleep.

Why did the girl take the pencil to bed?
To draw the curtains.

What's the difference between a soldier and a fireman?
You can't dip a fireman in your egg.

What do you call a man who plays with leaves?
Russell.

What do you call a man with a seagull on its head?
Cliff.

What do you call a man who comes through your letterbox?
Bill.

What do you call a man with a spade in his hand?
Doug.

What do you call a man without a spade in his hand?
Douglas.

What's the world's fastest cake?
Scone.

What's black, white and red all over?
A zebra wearing too much lipstick.

Bizarre Olympic sports

The 2008 Olympic Games, in Beijing, are the first to include BMX biking as a recognised sport. This isn't the same as mountain biking, which has been an official sport since way back in 1996. So how often are new sports added?

Fairly frequently, it turns out. The triathlon only made it onto the list in 2000, four years after softball and 16 years after synchronised swimming. The International Olympic Committee will consider any sport that it considers both geographically widespread and popular enough.

Once a sport is on the list, though, it isn't guaranteed a permanent place. Sports which have fallen from favour include croquet and cricket (both last placed in 1900), polo (1936), golf (1904) and the tug of war (1920).

The 1904 tug of war finals (pictured above), staged in the United States, were won by the United States. The silver medal went to the United States, and the bronze medal to, er, the United States. Clearly, knowledge of the terrain is the key to success in this sport: at the following Olympic Games, held in London in 1908, the gold medal went to Great Britain (City of London Police), the silver to Great Britain (Liverpool Police) and the bronze to Great Britain (Metropolitan Police K Division). The IOC decided the whole thing was too dodgy for its own good.

The 1904 Olympics were quite bizarre. In order to include 'primitive' tribes – Patagonians, Pygmies and so on – events included mud fighting, rock and spear throwing, and greasy pole climbing. It was such an embarrassment that these sports were immediately dropped from the competition.

Interested parties are currently lobbying the IOC to make paintball an official sport at the 2012 games in London. Britain's contribution to world culture has never looked so shaky.

10 Let me explain...

WHICH CAME FIRST, the chicken or the egg? It's a puzzle that has baffled some of the brightest brains on the planet. Well, okay, it's a puzzle that has baffled some of the brightest *kids* on the planet.

But that's the whole point. No question is so daft that it won't have children endlessly puzzling over the answer. They're immersed in a complex world they barely understand; and when they get stuck, naturally they turn to Dad for help.

Unless you happen to be a science teacher, the chances are you'll be stuck on some of the trickier problems. So here are the solutions to some of the common questions kids might ask, as well as a few useful facts to spice up the conversation.

If you *do* know how something works, then be sure to steer the conversation in that direction so that your apparently bottomless fund of fascinating information can get an outing. You should aim to give your kids the impression that the explanations you've learnt in this chapter are just the tip of the vast iceberg of your knowledge: they need to come to believe that you know just about everything.

Why can't people be twice the size?

It's a staple of science fiction movies: spiders the size of elephants, people twelve feet tall, horses shrunk to the size of mice. But is it possible?

In a word, no. There's a good reason why spiders have thin spindly legs, while elephants have great thick chunky ones. It's all to do with how length, area and volume get bigger at different rates.

Imagine you have a square Lego brick, with four bobbles on top, that's approximately a centimetre on each side.

Now let's make a brick that's twice as big as this one. That is, it's twice as high, twice as wide, and twice as deep. We end up with an assembly like the one shown on the left.

The height is double the size of the single brick. Look at the top face: that's four times the size of the single brick. Count the number of bricks we've used, and you'll see that doubling all the dimensions has given us a volume that's *eight times* what we started out with.

Now imagine a ball hanging from a thread, so that the thread is just strong enough to support it. If the ball were any heavier, the thread would break. Let's double the size of the ball and the thread.

As we've seen, if the ball's twice as big, its volume will be eight times as much, so it will weigh eight times as much. And what of the thread? It will be twice as wide, twice as deep and twice as long.

Except that being twice as long doesn't make it any stronger; in fact, the thread will only be four times as thick, just as the top surface of the Lego assembly is four times the area of the original brick. So the thread will break.

So it is with people. If we were double the size, we'd be eight times the weight, but our muscles would only be four times as strong. And if a spider were, say, a hundred times the size, it would weigh a million times more (100 x 100 x 100), but its legs could carry only ten thousand times as much (100 x 100). Like super-sized people, it would simply collapse under its own weight.

Why haven't we been visited by aliens?

It's a good question. After all, the universe is vast, and the chance of there being some intelligent life out there can't be all that small. So why have none of them made it here yet?

There's a good explanation, and it goes like this. First, ask your child to think how fast a supercharged alien rocket could travel. A thousand miles an hour? A hundred thousand miles an hour? OK, let's assume our alien rocket is so advanced it can travel at a *million* miles an hour. That's pretty fast.

But it's not fast enough. The nearest star to us is Proxima Centauri, which is also the nearest place there could possibly be planets that might support life. And it's 4.2 light years away. Which, put another way, is rather over 24 trillion miles (that's 24,000,000,000,000). So even if our aliens travelled at a million miles an hour, it would still take them nearly three thousand years to get here.

Even for aliens that's an awfully long journey, just on the off chance that we happened to be in when they called.

Why don't people have four arms?

Kids should ask questions: it's a sign of an active and enquiring mind. Sometimes, though, they'll ask a question that has no answer – because the questioner is starting from an impossible situation.

Typical questions might be: 'If people could breathe underwater, would we have gills instead of nostrils?'; 'If they managed to invent a camera that could photograph things that hadn't happened yet, would that mean you couldn't stop the things from happening?' – and so on. And on.

We have a standard response to this sort of question. It takes the form of another question: 'If dolphins had wings, would they speak Swahili?' Usually, this is enough to indicate that their original question is unanswerable.

How do seatbelts work?

We use them every day, and at some point it crosses most children's minds that their behaviour is actually rather odd. When you move slowly, they wind in and out freely; but when you move fast, they lock up. How is this achieved?

They're called 'inertial seatbelts', and they work on the principle of centrifugal force. The precise mechanism varies between designs, but here's the basic idea.

Imagine an arm, pivoted at the middle, which spins as you pull the seatbelt. On each end of the arm are weights, held into the centre by springs; there are teeth around the outside:

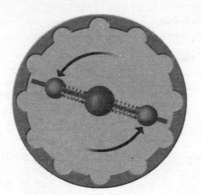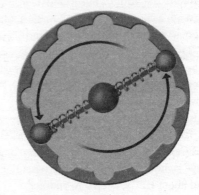

When the belt is pulled slowly (left), the weights stay near the centre – they're pulled there by the springs. But when the belt is pulled quickly (right), centrifugal force makes the weights fly to the outside. They lock into the teeth, preventing the hub from turning, and so preventing the seatbelt from pulling any further.

How do dimmer switches work?

Dimmer switches used to work by passing the current through a variable resistor, which would reduce the amount actually reaching the bulb. The trouble is, all that power had to go somewhere – and it went into heating up the resistor. Which meant that not only did the switch itself get very hot, which was pretty dangerous, it also cost you the same as keeping the bulb on full brightness.

These days, dimmer switches work by turning the bulb on and off, many times a second. The longer the bulb is off, the dimmer it is. Simple, but brilliant – or dim, if that's the setting you prefer.

How do fridges work?

When a liquid evaporates, it gets loses heat. That's why you feel cold when you get out of a swimming pool, even on a summer's day: the water evaporating from your skin cools you down.

Fridges use this process using a gas which liquifies at a very low temperature. This flows in a zigzag tube through the fridge; you can see the ripples in the back and roof. The cold gas flows through the fridge, absorbing heat; it then goes through a compressor, which turns it into a liquid as it goes through a similar zigzag tube on the outside of the fridge, at the back. A fan blows through this tube, blowing the absorbed heat away; the liquid then goes through an expansion gate, which turns it back into a gas, cooling it down so it can absorb more heat.

In the early days, ammonia was the gas of choice. But it's toxic, and after a number of fatal accidents manufacturers switched to chloroflurocarbons (CFCs). Then they discovered those damaged the ozone layer, and have switched to hydroflurocarbons (HFCs). If you know anything bad about HFCs, keep it to yourself.

How do electric toothbrushes work?

When you recharge your phone, your iPod or your digital camera, you can see the metal contacts that join the device to the charger. Rechargeable toothbrushes, however, don't have any visible contacts: bare metal, with current flowing through it, would be far too dangerous to keep in a bathroom.

Instead, the transformer that provides the power to the batteries in the toothbrush is split into two halves. One coil and a metal rod are in the charger, the other coil is inside the toothbrush itself. Since transformers work using magnetic forces, the two coils don't need to be touching, as long as they're close to each other. When you place the toothbrush into the charger, it completes the transformer, so charging can take place.

Which came first, the chicken or the egg?

It's an old problem. The chicken had to come from an egg; but the egg had to come from a chicken. Or did it?

Chickens evolved, just as people evolved. So there must have been a first chicken, before which it was a jurassic chickenosaurus, or some such pseudo scientific nonsense.

But there were eggs long before there were chickens. Dinosaurs hatched from eggs. So our very first proto-chicken must have come from an egg; but the egg itself came from the immediate ancestor of the chicken. Problem solved!

How does Google work?

Google is such an advanced search engine that it's just about beaten all the rest into submission. It can be startlingly accurate. But how does it locate pages so quickly, among the many millions out there?

Google uses a network of thousands of ordinary PCs, constantly scanning the web and cataloguing each page it comes across. But the really clever part is how it judges how significant each page is.

Let's say you set up your own home page. Google will find it eventually, and catalogue every word on it. But why does a reference on your page come so far down the list, compared with references to the same word on better known sites? The answer is that Google ranks the 'value' of your page depending on how many other pages link to it. Not just that, but more significant pages linking to yours will have a higher ranking: so if your page is mentioned in your friend's blog, it won't score very highly; if it's referred to on *The Guardian* website, it will up your ranking significantly.

Yes, but how do Google make any money out of it?

Let's say you search for 'digital cameras'. Down the right of the results page you'll see half a dozen links to digital camera sites. These links are bid for by people wanting to advertise: Google doesn't set the rates, it's simply the highest bidders who get a listing here. Each time you click on one of those links, the advertiser will pay Google a dollar or so for the privilege of getting your attention.

It's come down to a fine art. Buying Adwords for 'digital camera' searches will cost around a dollar: Adwords for 'digital cameras' searches cost double that. Someone, somewhere, has worked out that people searching for 'digital cameras' end up buying one. It's a fine art, advertising.

How fast do things fall?

Acceleration due to gravity, as we learnt at school, is 9.8 metres per second squared. Come again? Well, there's a simple way to work out how many seconds it takes a dropped object to hit the ground: double the height in metres, divide by 9.8 and then take the square root. Easier if you have a calculator to hand!

Of course, there are minor things like air resistance to take into account, so this formula won't work for very big distances, or very light objects. But here's a visual guide to some useful distances:

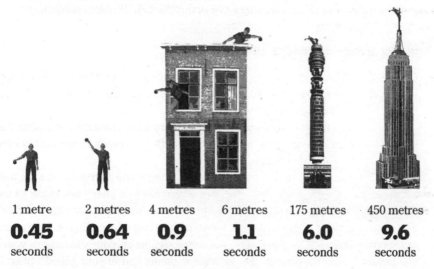

1 metre	2 metres	4 metres	6 metres	175 metres	450 metres
0.45 seconds	**0.64** seconds	**0.9** seconds	**1.1** seconds	**6.0** seconds	**9.6** seconds

Why doesn't the Moon crash into the Earth?

In fact, the Moon *is* constantly falling towards the Earth. But the surface of the Earth, being curved, falls away from the Moon at exactly the same rate. If the Moon moved slower, or faster, it would either crash into us or fly off into space.

It's the same as the reason why satellites don't fall down. They're pushed at exactly the right speed to keep them at a uniform distance above the Earth. If the satellite is positioned at exactly 26,240 miles above the Earth, it will stay precisely above the same spot on the Earth's surface: these satellites are in what's called geosynchronous orbit, which is how we can pick up satellite TV without having to keep moving the dish.

Why Fahrenheit and Celsius?

In 1724, Gabriel Fahrenheit measured the lowest temperature he could achieve, and called that 0°. He decided there should be 180° between the freezing point and the boiling point of water, perhaps to mimic the 180° in a semicircle: and so ended up with 32° for the freezing point, and 212° for the boiling point.

In 1742 Anders Celsius decided this was a stupid system, and devised a better one based purely around water. In his system, water boiled at 0°, and froze at 100°. Yes, that's right. It wasn't until someone pointed out the supreme idiocy of this approach that it was changed to water freezing at 0° and boiling at 100°. Originally called centigrade, the scale was renamed Celsius to commemorate him.

So what's absolute zero, then?

In 1848, scientist Lord Kelvin decided to see at what temperature the molecules in various gases would stop moving. To his surprise, they all stopped at the same temperature: minus 273°C. He figured out that this was a complete absence of heat: absolute zero, the lowest temperature there is.

A famous piece of music by the American composer John Cage, called 4'33", consists of total silence that lasts for that period of time. 4 minutes 33 seconds is, of course, 273 seconds.

How do 3D glasses work?

The first 3D film was *The Power of Love*, made in 1922. Sadly, the film dropped out of circulation, and there are no known copies still in existence. But film makers have been churning out 3D movies, with varying degrees of success, ever since. The 3D effect depends on our ability to see different images with each eye.

Red and green lenses: There are two main ways of making 3D images and films. The simplest uses red and green lenses, one for each eye. When looking through the red lens, everything looks red – so anything that actually *is* red will be invisible. Anything that's green, on the other hand, will appear black, because green is the 'opposite' colour to red; the same works, in reverse, with the other lens.

You can simulate the effect using the red and green transparent wrappers from Quality Street chocolates. Draw a face on a sheet of paper using a red felt pen or crayon; draw an identical face about a centimetre away, so the two overlap, using a green pen. When you hold the wrappers over your eyes, each one will filter out that colour, and you'll see a face that appears to hover above the page.

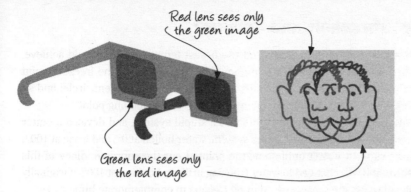

Red lens sees only the green image

Green lens sees only the red image

Polarized lenses: The trouble with red and green lenses is that you can only see things in black and white. For full colour, you need to split an image so that each eye sees a completely different image. Polarized lenses, of the sort used in sunglasses, are made with imperceptible straight lines on them. If the lines are vertical, and you look at an image made of vertical lines, you won't see anything – but you will see an image made of horizontal lines, and vice versa. So colour movies place two images on top of each other, one made of vertical lines, one of horizontal, and the glasses filter out each image.

You can show how this works by taking two pairs of sunglasses and placing them together so you're looking through both lenses at once. When they're arranged so the lines are at right angles to each other, you'll be able to see through them; but rotate one pair by 90° so they line up and they'll go totally opaque, as the lines coincide to cut out all the light.

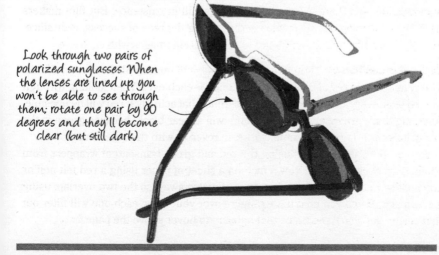

Look through two pairs of polarized sunglasses. When the lenses are lined up, you won't be able to see through them; rotate one pair by 90 degrees and they'll become clear (but still dark)

How are cranes put up?

Although a common sight in most cities, you rarely see the multiplicity of cranes that tower hundreds of feet up in the air actually being put up. They just seem to appear overnight. How does it happen? Do you need a bigger crane to put a smaller crane up and an even bigger one to get that one up? In that case, how did the world's biggest crane go up?

Cranes on building sites are usually tower cranes. Tower cranes usually *are* initially built by smaller, weaker cranes, either mobile cranes or telescopic tower types. But once the main crane outgrows them, they have to put themselves up. A cradle encircling the tower hydraulically jacks up the crane, enabling the crane to winch up the next section of the mast, which is fitted into position and bolted into place. Then it does it again, and again, each time the cab and jib (or arm) getting further and further from the ground.

A standalone tower crane is usually no higher than 80 metres (265 feet) and can lift a maximum of 20 tonnes (the same as three African elephants), though this decreases the further out along the arm the load goes. However, cranes can go higher and lift more if they are fastened onto the buildings they are helping to erect, often being situated in what will eventually be the lift shaft. The world's largest tower cranes, the Danish K10000, stand 120 metres high (almost three

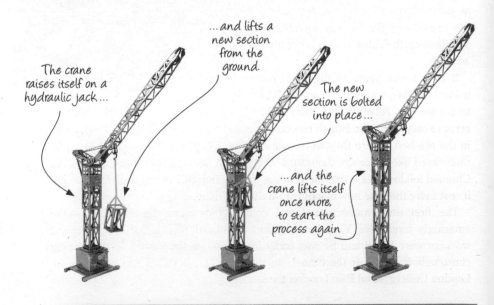

The crane raises itself on a hydraulic jack...

...and lifts a new section from the ground.

The new section is bolted into place...

...and the crane lifts itself once more, to start the process again times the height of the Statue of Liberty). The jib is 100 metres, it has a service crane all of its own on top, can lift a maximum of 360 tonnes and even has a lift for those who have to go up it.

Children often wonder why cranes don't topple over, particularly in high winds. They are anchored with massive bolts to concrete which has been poured into the ground and there are heavy counterweights on the rear of the jib. If the wind rises to more than 40 or 50 miles an hour, cranes have to stop working and they are left to 'weathervane', swinging with the wind so that the jib points in the same direction as the wind is blowing. Cranes in Europe are supposed to be able to survive winds of 100 miles an hour.

Incredibly large mobile cranes also exist. The UK has two of the largest currently made, the Terex Demag AC 700. This telescopic crane can rise to 133 metres when fully extended and can lift a staggering 700 tonnes.

Tunnels are boring? Not!

Tunnels such as the Channel Tunnel are constructed by giant tunnel boring machines (TBMs) which have giant circular cutting wheels at the front. They use the same principle as earthworms to progress, expanding to grip the tunnel and dig its way forward, and then withdrawing the sides so the rear of the TBM can advance.

It took seven years to dig the Channel Tunnel using 11 TBMs. It's 30 miles long with 24 miles actually under the sea. After the two pairs of TBMs met in the middle in 1991 (with an error of only 2cm), the British machines turned off course and buried themselves in the sea bed, where they were concreted in. They're still there, waiting to be discovered like space age dinosaurs. The French decided to dismantle theirs but Chunnel folklore has it that the process was so time-consuming and difficult that it cost more than the new machines would have done.

The first underwater tunnel was constructed under the Thames by the amazingly innovative Victorian engineer Isambard Kingdom Brunel. Several workers were killed and he was badly injured when the tunnel flooded during construction. However the tunnel, finished in 1843, is still in use today by the London Underground East London Line.

Why is the sky black at night?

It's not as daft a question as it might sound. There's no Sun to light it up – but there are billions of suns out there, all shining away. So why isn't the sky dazzling white? The further away the stars are, the more their light diminishes before reaching us; but then the further the distance, the more stars there are around us. This is known as Olbers' Paradox, after the mathematician who was first puzzled by it.

The answer is surprising. If the universe were infinitely old, then all the light in it would have had time to reach everywhere, and the night sky would be bright. But the universe isn't infinitely old, so a lot of the light is still on its way. Come back in a couple of zillion years and ask the question again.

What's so clever about ballpoint pens?

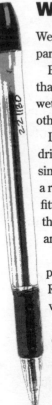

We use them every day, and lose them every other day. They've become so much part of the furniture that we tend to forget how ingenious they really are.

Before they were invented, people wrote with fountain pens. The problem was that if the ink was wet enough not to dry up as it flowed down the nib, it remained wet on the paper – which is the main reason why people owned blotters. (The other reason was to provide clues for Hercule Poirot.)

Laszlo Bíró was a journalist who saw a newspaper being printed with ink that dried as soon as it hit the paper, and determined to devise a method for using a similar quick-drying ink in pen form. But printing ink is too thick to flow through a regular pen. His ingenious solution was a ball that held the ink in its tube, which fitted just well enough to allow a thin film of the ink to roll on to the paper when the pen was used. The mechanism is the same as that used in roll-on deodorants, and in fact their invention was inspired by the biro.

Laszlo and his brother Georg took out a patent on the device in 1943; the patent was bought by the British government, so they could supply pilots in the RAF with pens that didn't leak ink at high altitude. The only problem was, they were extremely expensive to make.

In 1945, the Frenchman Marcel Bich invented a manufacturing process to enable him to make ballpoint pens cheaply. He named them Bic, after himself. They were a phenomenal success: in 2005, the company he founded sold its *hundred billionth* ballpoint pen. That's more than 15 pens for each man, woman and child on the planet.

So where the hell are they all, then?

11 Language stuff

FROM THE MOMENT THEY BEGIN to talk, kids start to learn to argue. It's a sad fact of life that we wait years for them to be old enough to hold an intelligent conversation, then spend the rest of our lives waiting for them to shut up.

Kids have an insatiable appetite for new words, continually questioning our speech and asking for definitions of new concepts. But language is much more than a means of everyday conversation: words can be endlessly fascinating, and kids have the ability to latch on to the more obscure words simply because they like the sound they make.

Our language is riddled with peculiar and odd words, from the longest word in English to the longest domain name, from the names for collectors of beermats to the name of the fear of getting peanut butter stuck to the roof of your mouth.

Here's a selection of the interesting, the factual, the absurd, and the downright idiotic to keep them amused. We've also thrown in a few nonsense verses which are fun to learn, and make useful alternatives to bedtime stories.

A for 'orses

This comic rendering of the alphabet has been around, in one form or another, for a century or more. We've put together the best of the variations, and added a few of our own when the originals have seemed a little long in the tooth.

If you don't get what's going on here, try saying them aloud. If you *still* don't get what's going on, ask your kids to help you out.

A for 'orses
B for Veggie burgers
C for Miles
D for Rent
E for Ning All
F for Vescent
G for Police
H for Retirement
I for Knock knock joke for you
J for Cakes
K for Teria
L for Leather
M for Sis
N for Lope
O for the Rainbow
P for Ming Seals
Q for a Bus
R for Mo
S for You
T for Two
U for Mystic
V for La France
W for Quits
X for Breakfast
Y for Runts
Z for a Doctor, I got a code in me dose

A, I'm adorable,
B, I'm beautiful...

Nonsense verse

There's no point whatsoever to these little ditties. Except, of course, that they're fun to say to your kids.

One day next week at break of night
I met a dog whose wings were white.
He bit my tail, I pinched his fins
We fought right through the darkest light.

I shot him with my rubber sword
He opened wide his ears and roared.
He looked me squarely in the nose
And strangled me with a piano chord.

'Why are we fighting?' I whispered loud,
As snow rained from the mushroom cloud.
He answered that he could not speak –
The rule is clear: 'No dogs aloud.'

I laughed a sneer, my blood ran red:
He raised his gun and sliced off my head.
I ate him then, his feathers and all
And we lay there panting, both stone dead.

One day next week as the sun grew dark
I fought like a dog, he sang like a shark.
And when at last the fight was done
I killed him with my question mark.

Algy met a bear.
The bear met Algy.
The bear was bulgy.
The bulge was Algy.

The elephant is a bonnie bird,
It flits from bough to bough,
It makes its nest in the rhubarb tree,
And whistles like a cow.

Trade names

It used to be common practice to refer to vacuum cleaners as Hoovers. Which was immensely annoying for Hoover, who go to great lengths to correct anyone who misuses their trademarked name in print.

All the words below are now so much part of the language that you'd be forgiven for thinking they were generic terms. In fact the only people who probably won't forgive you are the lawyers of the companies who own them:

Astro Turf	*Band-Aid*	*Breathalyzer*	*Brillo Pads*	*Dumpster*
Frisbee	*Hoover*	*Hula-Hoop*	*Jacuzzi*	*Jeep*
Kleenex	*Laundromat*	*Magic Marker*	*Muzak*	*Novocaine*
Ping-Pong	*Play-Doh*	*Post-it note*	*Q-Tip*	*Rollerblade*
Scotch Tape	*Scrabble*	*Sellotape*	*Styrofoam*	*Super Glue*
Technicolor	*Teflon*	*TelePrompter*	*Vaseline*	*Velcro*
Walkman	*Xerox*			

Sometimes common sense wins out over legal argument. The following words all *used* to be trademarks, but have now been ruled part of the language:

aspirin	*bikini*	*brassiere*	*cellophane*	*dry ice*
escalator	*gramophone*	*gunk*	*kiwi fruit*	*linoleum*
petrol	*pilates*	*plasterboard*	*shredded wheat*	*tabloid*
thermos	*touch-tone*	*trampoline*	*yo-yo*	*zip*

Q here

Are there are any English words where a 'u' doesn't follow a 'q'? Yes, though you aren't likely to be using them every day. *Qadi* is a Muslim judge; *qigong* is a Chinese system of physical exercises; *qin*, a Chinese musical instrument; *qintar*, money in Albania, worth $\frac{1}{100}$ of a lek; *qwerty*, the layout of typewriter and computer keyboards; and *suq*, an Arab marketplace.

What comes after 'once', 'twice' and 'thrice'?

Sadly, there's nothing after that. Quince is a fruit you can make into marmalade but it has nothing to do with five.

Got a fear? Get a phobia

This selection of phobias includes several that bright children could carefully employ instead of claiming that 'the dog ate my homework'.

Ablutophobia . . . . Fear of washing or bathing
Achluophobia . . . . Fear of darkness
Acousticophobia . . . . Fear of noise
Agliophobia . . . . Fear of pain
Ambulophobia . . . . Fear of walking
Apiphobia . . . . Fear of bees
Arachibutyrophobia . . . . . Fear of peanut butter sticking to the roof of the mouth
Autodysomophobia . . . . . . Fear of someone who has a vile odour
Bibliophobia . . . . Fear of books
Chronomentrophobia . . . . Fear of clocks
Cibophobia . . . . Fear of food (also called Sitophobia and Sitiophobia)
Clinophobia . . . . Fear of going to bed
Decidophobia . . . . Fear of making decisions
Deipnophobia . . . . Fear of dining or dinner conversations
Dentophobia . . . . Fear of dentists
Didaskaleinophobia . . . . . Fear of going to school
Entomophobia . . . . Fear of insects
Eosophobia . . . . Fear of dawn or daylight
Ephebiphobia . . . . Fear of teenagers
Epistemophobia . . . . Fear of knowledge
Ergophobia . . . . Fear of work
Gnosiophobia . . . . Fear of knowledge
Hypnophobia . . . . Fear of sleep (or of being hypnotised)
Iatrophobia . . . . Fear of going to the doctor
Ichthyophobia . . . . Fear of fish
Kathisophobia . . . . Fear of sitting down
Logophobia . . . . Fear of words
Numerophobia . . . . Fear of numbers
Odontophobia . . . . Fear of teeth or dental surgery
Poinephobia . . . . Fear of punishment
Ponophobia . . . . Fear of overworking or of pain
Sophophobia . . . . Fear of learning

Tongue-twisters

Almost every language has combinations of sounds that can be hard to say, though tongue-twisters are often so nonsensical there would normally be no reason to say them except as a challenge. In English, the most difficult tongue-twister is said to be 'The sixth sick sheikh's sixth sheep's sick' – which we finally mastered, only to discover that some sadist has since added 'so six slick sheiks sold six sick sheep six silk sheets'.

But that's not to say we don't enjoy tongue-twisters and competing with our kids to see who can say them best. Here are some of our favourites. The shorter ones need to be repeated several times, if indeed that is possible.

Sixish
Big boat
Toy whip
Truly rural
Greek grapes
Ed had edited it
Irish wristwatch
Unique New York
Three free throws
Cheap sheep soup
Preshrunk silk shirts
Three boys felt smart
Aluminium Ambulance
Shredded Swiss cheese
Quick kiss, quicker kiss
The myth of Miss Muffet
Plague-bearing prairie dogs
Mrs Smith's Fish Sauce Shop
The soldier's shoulder surely hurts
Plain bun, plum bun, bun without plum
A box of biscuits, a batch of mixed biscuits
Fred fed Ted bread, and Ted fed Fred bread
What time does the wristwatch strap shop shut?
Give papa a proper cup of coffee in a proper coffee cup
Betty and Bob brought back blue balloons from the big bazaar

We find selling seashells and picking pecks of pickled peppers tedious, so we're only including one longer one. As it offers such practical advice, you may want to master it, ready for the day when you can finally usefully use it.

You've no need to light a night-light
On a light night like tonight.
For a night-light's light's a slight light
And tonight's a night that's light.
When a night's light, like tonight's light,
It is really not quite right
To light night-lights with their slight lights,
On a light night like tonight.

Of all the French tongue-twisters we looked at, dictionary in hand, this was about the only one we could understand: 'Dans ta tente ta tante t'attend' which means 'In your tent, your aunt is waiting for you.'

In German, which we found tricky enough when we had to study it at school, this is one of the most popular tongue-twisters: 'Brautkleid bleibt Brautkleid und Blaukraut bleibt Blaukraut'. It's pretty nonsensical, meaning 'A wedding dress will be a wedding dress and red cabbage will be red cabbage'.

Musical words

Any number of words can be made using the letters A to G used in musical notation: everyday words such as ACE, DEAF, BED, BAG and so on may sound awkward when played, but it's possible to construct a reasonable tune. There are even some seven letter words, including BAGGAGE, DEFACED and FEEDBAG. Of course, the best word to play is DAD, we're sure you'll agree.

If you have musically inclined kids, here's a little puzzle you can show them – or even play to them, should they happen to have perfect pitch. Can they decipher the words?

All dogs go woof

Or do they? Not according to Professor Catherine Ball, who has collected the sounds made by dogs in different languages around the world. For more animal sounds, from bees to zebras, visit her website at http://www.georgetown.edu/faculty/ballc/animals/animals.html.

Afrikaans	woef	Hindi	bho-bho
Albanian	ham ham	Hungarian	vau-vau
Arabic	haw haw	Icelandic	voff
Bengali	ghaue-ghaue	Indonesian	gonggong
Catalan	bup, bup	Italian	bau bau
Chinese	wang wang	Japanese	kyankyan
Croatian	vau-vau	Korean	mung-mung
Danish	vov	Norwegian	vov-vov
Dutch	woef	Polish	hau hau
English	woof woof	Portuguese	au-au
Old English	Hund byrcð	Russian	gav-gav
Esperanto	boj	Slovene	hov-hov
Estonian	auh	Spanish	guau guau
Finnish	hau hau	Swedish	vov vov
French	ouah ouah	Thai	hoang hoang
German	wau wau	Turkish	hav, hav
Greek	gav	Ukrainian	haf-haf
Hebrew	haw haw	Vietnamese	wau wau

wang wang

hov-hov

boj

How 2 txt yr kids

Just when you thought you'd got the hang of the whole hip, cool world of teenage slang, along came texting – and instant messaging – with their own set of rules and abbreviations. If your kids are old enough to have their own mobile phones, here's how you can communicate with them in their own language.

Don't just miss out every vowel: this is a misunderstanding caused by advertising agencies who want to look cool, and you'll be marked down as a wannabe yoof the moment you start. Instead, miss out the final 'e' on words like 'give' and 'some'. Words should be spelled phonetically where it saves space: so use 'luv' for 'love', 'ne' for 'any', 'b' for 'be', and so on.

Wherever possible, replace a combination of letters with numbers or symbols that sound the same. So 'great' becomes 'gr8', 'hand' becomes 'h&', 'tomorrow' becomes '2moro', 'before' becomes 'b4'.

Miss out words that aren't absolutely essential to the sense of the sentence. A sentence like 'Are you OK? You forgot to take your skates with you' can be quickly sent as 'u k? u 4gt yr sk8s', which takes much less time to type.

There's also a wide range of codes used both for texting and IM chatting. Some are less well known: you might think 'wombat' is a great abbreviation for 'waste of money, brains and time' but it's unlikely your kids will get it. Here's a list of the more common shortenings:

are you OK?	ruok/u k	later	l8r
as far as I know	afaik	laugh out loud/lots of love	lol
all my love	aml	message	msg
be seeing you	bcnu	mind your own business	myob
because	bcz	no problem	np
be right back	brb	people	ppl
by the way	btw	please	plz
don't know	dno	please call me	pcm
for what it's worth	fwiw	please write back	pwb
got to go	gtg	see you later	cul8r
have a good one	hago	straight	str8
in my opinion	imo	thank you	ty
instant message	im	thanks	thx
keep it simple, stupid	kiss	well done	wd
kiss	x	with	w
know	kno	your	yr

What is the longest word in English?

Most of the supposedly 'longest' words in the English language are made up in order to get into lists of the longest words in the English language, such as this one. According to the Oxford dictionary people, the longest genuine words are:

pseudopseudohypoparathyroidism	30	A disorder with similar symptoms to pseudohypoparathyroidism
floccinaucinihilipilification	29	The act of estimating something as worthless
antidisestablishmentarianism	28	The view opposing the idea that the Church of England and the state should be separated

The Oxford dictionaries also list *pneumonoultramicroscopicsilicovolcanoconiosis* (45 letters), apparently a lung disease, but it was almost certainly invented simply to be a long word. Often quoted as the longest are the formal names of chemical compounds which can be almost unlimited in length. Some have been written out with over 1000 letters. But they aren't real words.

The song *Supercalifragilisticexpialidocious* (34 letters) from Mary Poppins is listed in some dictionaries. You're unlikely to find *Lip-smackin-thirst-quenchin-acetastin-motivatin-good-buzzin-cool-talkin-high-walkin-fast-livin-ever-givincool-fizzin* listed, but that's the 100-letter concatenated 'word' from a 1973 Pepsi ad that loads of dads will still remember.

The *humuhumu-nukunuku-a-pua'a* (22 letters) is Hawaii's official state fish, otherwise known as a reef triggerfish. Some say that the name is longer than the fish itself.

Longest place names

Llanfairpwllgwyngyllgogerychwyrndrobwllllantysiliogogogoch in Anglesey, Wales, with 58 letters, is often said to be the longest place name in Britain. In Welsh the name means 'St Mary's Church in the hollow of the white hazel near to the rapid whirlpool of Llantysilio of the red cave'. In fact, the long version of the town's real name of Llanfairpwllgwyngyll (sometimes just called 'Llanfair PG') was made up in the 19th century as a publicity stunt. Nonetheless several shops and the railway station display the sign in full.

To say the name, you'll need to know that the Welsh *ll* is pronounced as the Scots do the ch of loch. Make this noise, seguing into *lan – vire – pu* (as in put) – *ll* again – *gwin – gil* (like fish gill), segueing into *ll – go* (o as in dog) – *ger – uch* (with the ch as in Scottish loch) – *win – drawb – u* (as in put) – *ll – llan* (as at beginning) – *ti – silly – o – go – go – go – ll*.

There's a joke about two English speakers asking the person serving them food in Llanfair PG if she can say the name of the place they're in very slowly. 'Certainly,' she says, 'it's M-a-c-d-o-n-a-l-d-s.'

Trying to beat the record for the longest Welsh name, somebody recently came up with *Gorsafawddachaidraigodanheddogleddolonpenrhynareurdraethceredigion*, which has 66 letters against 53 ('ll' only counts as one letter in Welsh) and means 'the Mawddach station and its dragon teeth at the Northern Penrhyn Road on the golden beach of Cardigan bay'. It hasn't taken off.

Longest internet name: The longest internet domain name in the world is probably *llanfairpwllgwyngyllgogerychwyrndrobwllllantysiliogogogochuchaf.org.uk*, which is the name reserved for the upper part of the village. But there are several other contenders for the dubious title of the longest .com domain names, including *thelongestdomainnameintheworldandthensomeandthensomemoreandmore.com* and *Iamtheproudownerofthelongestlongestlongestdomainnameinthisworld.com*.

Longest place name: The longest name in common usage is an 82-letter hill in New Zealand. *Taumatawhakatangihangakoauotamateturipukakapikimaungahor o-Nukupokaiwhenuakitanatahu* apparently means 'the place where Tamatea, the man with the big knees, who slid, climbed and swallowed mountains, known as land-eater, played his flute to his loved one'.

Longest lake name: There are a mere 45 letters in the Massachusetts lake which revels in the name *Chargoggagoggmanchauggagoggchaubunagungamaugg*, though that does include 9 A's and 15 G's. Locals, who often can't spell it, have simply taken to calling it Webster Lake after the local town.

Collecting the collectors

Shells, stamps, coins, books – we all know people who collect one or more of these items. But what of the collectors of packets of sugar, car tax discs and thimbles? Such people do exist. And they not only have websites, they also have names: for each bizarre collectible, there's an equally bizarre name to describe those who collect them. Here are a few of our favourites:

Aerophilately	air mail stamps and covers
Archtophilist	teddy bears
Argyrothecologist	money boxes
Bestiarist	medieval books on animals
Brandophilist	cigar bands
Cartophilist	cigarette cards
Conchologist	shells
Copoclephilist	keyrings
Deltiologist	postcards
Digitabulist	thimbles
Fusilatelist	telephone calling cards
Helixophilist	corkscrews
Labeorphilist	beer bottle labels
Lepidopterist	butterflies
Lotologist	scratchcards and lottery items
Notaphilist	banknotes
Numismatist	coins
Philatelist	stamps
Phillumenist	matchbox labels
Philographist	autographs
Plangonologist	dolls
Receptarist	recipes
Rhykenologist	woodworking tools
Scripophilist	old financial documents
Succrologist	sugar packets
Tegestologist	beer mats
Tyrosemiophilist	cheese labels
Vecturist	underground and other transport tokens
Velologist	vehicle excise licences (tax discs)
Vexillologist	banners or flags

Pangrams

Pangrams are sentences containing all the letters of the alphabet. The most well known is 'The quick brown fox jumps over the lazy dog', and it's often used to show all the characters in a typeface. Here are some others:

A mad boxer shot a quick, gloved jab to the jaw of his dizzy opponent.
About sixty codfish eggs will make a quarter pound of very fizzy jelly.
Astronaut Quincy B. Zack defies gravity with six jet fuel pumps.
Barkeep! A flaming tequila swizzle and a vodka and Ajax, hold the cherry.
Five jumbo oxen graze quietly with packs of dogs.
Five or six big jet planes zoomed quickly by the tower.
Fred specialized in the job of making very quaint wax toys.
How quickly daft jumping zebras vex.
I have quickly spotted the four women dozing in the jury box.
Jack amazed a few girls by dropping the antique onyx vase.
Jolly housewives made inexpensive meals using quick-frozen vegetables.
Quiz explained for TV show by Mick Jagger.
Six of the women quietly gave back prizes to the judge.
The five boxing wizards jump quickly.
Up at the zoo a roving ox was quickly fed bug jam.
Wolves exit quickly as fanged zoo chimp jabbers.
Woven silk pyjamas exchanged for blue quartz.

How many words in the English language?

The Oxford dictionary people say it's impossible to answer this definitively but suggest that there are at least a quarter of a million distinct English words, with perhaps 20 per cent no longer in current use. It's also believed that English has as many words as French, German and Spanish put together.

The most common nouns in English are, in order: Time, Person, Year, Way, Day, Thing, Man, World, Life and Hand. 90 per cent of the top 100 words used in English are only one syllable and, despite the rapidity with which new words are coined, most of the most popular words we use every day date back to before the Norman Conquest (1066).

The language teacher Michel Thomas reckons that most people only use between 500 and 1,500 words.

Longest and shortest

What is the longest word in English of only one syllable? We can't do better than nine letters. These include 'screeched', 'scratched', 'scrounged', 'scrunched' and 'stretched', as well as 'straights' and 'strengths'.

The shortest word to contain the first six letters of the alphabet is 'feedback'.

Double meanings

Many words in the English language have more than one meaning. Normally, it's easy to tell which meaning is intended by the context. But sometimes it isn't quite so clear. Here are a few cases fraught with confusion:

Worrying: To 'worry' means to be overly concerned, often to the point of desperation. It also means to toy with something, as a cat does when it's playing with a mouse. So when a dog worries a sheep, is it the dog or the sheep that's doing the worrying?

Car parks: A park is a wide open space, often in the form of a garden. To park your car, on the other hand, means to leave it unattended. So is a car park a place where you park your car, or the space in which you leave it?

Sheer insanity: The word 'sheer' means 'transparent', when it's applied to stockings. It also means 'vertical' when it's applied to cliffs. So is sheer insanity transparent or vertical?

No way am I swallowing that, Mr Barrie

See you later, alligator

'Soon' means 'soon', and 'later' means 'later'. So why is it that when you say 'see you later' it generally means the same day, but when you say 'see you soon' it often means some time in the next few months?

Word quiz

1. Only five countries in the world have names of a single syllable. Which ones?

2. What's the first number to contain the letter 'a'?

3. What's the first number to contain the letter 'b'?

4. What's the only number with its letters in alphabetical order?

5. What links the words 'almost', 'begins' and 'chimps'?

6. What's the longest word you can type on the top row of letters on a computer keyboard?

7. Only one number can be spelled using the same number of letters as the number itself. What is it?

8. How does the number sequence 8 5 4 9 1 7 6 3 2 work?

9. The word 'skiing' has two dotted characters in a row. Which place name has three in a row?

10. What links the words 'polish', 'job', 'reading' and 'august'?

11. Can you think of a word that includes six consecutive consonants?

12. What links the words 'scissors', 'cattle' and 'clothes'?

13. What links the words 'cares', 'timelines' and 'princes'?

14. What links the words 'child', 'ox', 'man' and 'woman'?

15. Only one word in English ends in 'mt'. What is it?

16. Only two words in English end in 'gry'. What are they?

Answers

1. France, Spain, Greece, Laos and Chad. 2. One thousand. Or one hundred and one, if you prefer. 3. One billion. 4. Forty. 5. They have their letters in alphabetical order. 6. Typewriter. 7. Four. 8. The numbers are in alphabetical order. 9. Beijing and Fiji are the most well known. 10. They're pronounced differently when spelled with capital letters. 11. 'Watchstrap', 'catchphrase' and 'Knightsbridge' are the most common. 12. They're plural words that have no singular form. 13. They're plurals which become singular when an 's' is added on the end. 14. Their plurals end in -en. 15. Dreamt. 16. Angry and hungry.

Oops!

Never work
with children or
animals: sound
advice from W. C.
Fields. Here's a
selection of out-
takes from when
things didn't go
entirely according
to plan…

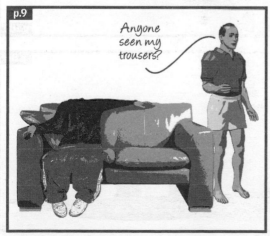

Your kids' birthdays

Name	Date	What to buy them

...and don't forget...

Your partner's birthday		
Your anniversary		

Other important notes

_____

_____

_____

Need more? Meet the authors and other Dads to suggest techniques,
exchange tips or just chat about the whole Dad thing:

www.dadstuff.co.uk